Sencha Charts Essentials

Create stunning charts and visualizations for both web
and mobile applications

Ajit Kumar

BIRMINGHAM - MUMBAI

Sencha Charts Essentials

First published: May 2015

Production reference: 1260515

Published by Packt Publishing Ltd.
Livery Place
35 Livery Street
Birmingham B3 2PB, UK.

ISBN 978-1-78528-976-7

www.packtpub.com

Credits

Author
Ajit Kumar

Reviewers
Anurag Bhandari
Peter M. Corcoran
Matt Goldspink
Shinobu Kawano
Michael McCurrey

Commissioning Editor
Veena Pagare

Acquisition Editor
Sam Wood

Content Development Editor
Anish Sukumaran

Technical Editors
Manal Pednekar
Chinmay S. Puranik

Copy Editor
Pranjali Chury

Project Coordinator
Izzat Contractor

Proofreaders
Stephen Copestake
Safis Editing

Indexer
Mariammal Chettiyar

Graphics
Disha Haria

Production Coordinator
Nilesh R. Mohite

Cover Work
Nilesh R. Mohite

About the Author

Ajit Kumar has over 16 years of experience in technology areas ranging from embedded systems to large enterprise applications. He worked with various multinational corporations such as Honeywell, Hughes, Virtusa, and Convergys, before starting his own company — Walking Tree — which specializes in Sencha frameworks.

Ajit has authored books on open source frameworks, including *Sencha Touch Cookbook*, *Sencha Touch Cookbook Second Edition*, *Sencha MVC Architecture*, and *ADempiere 3.6 Cookbook*, all by Packt Publishing, which he considers his way of thanking the awesome open source community!

I would like to thank my wife, Priti, for her untiring support and the great team at Packt Publishing for the wonderful authoring experience!

About the Reviewers

Anurag Bhandari is a web programmer and an open source evangelist. He has extensive experience in developing web applications, real-time web apps, and mobile apps. He's well-versed with several computer languages, such as C#, Java, PHP, Python, and JavaScript. Also, when it comes to languages, he speaks Hindi, Punjabi, and French. Being a technology enthusiast, he keeps meddling with trending technologies and trying out new frameworks and platforms. He has been heavily involved with open source Linux projects, OpenMandriva and Granular. He is also a bookworm, sports fan, gadget freak, philatelist, and movie buff. When not following any of his hobbies, he finds peace playing video games.

He hasn't technically reviewed any book before this one. However, he once wrote a general review of *Instant Meteor JavaScript Framework Starter*, *Packt Publishing*, on his blog.

> I'd like to congratulate Ajit Kumar on producing a comprehensive guide to creating beautiful charts and infographics using Sencha Charts. Ajit has put in great effort and hardwork to painstakingly cover even the minutest details of the framework. He has spent quality time on building both practical and aesthetically pleasing examples that you are bound to love and use in your own work.

Peter M. Corcoran has over 15 years of experience in innovative solution development, relationship building, and process and project management. In addition, he has a proven track record of analytical, technical, conceptual, and creative thinking skills, along with a strong commitment to customer service and support. He is currently working on an electrical engineering degree at the University of Alabama, Birmingham (his estimated graduation date is May 2016), and is a team leader of mobile application development at Regions Bank.

Peter started working with Sencha products in 2008 while working as a continuous service improvement analyst at the Southern Company. He built powerful web applications that helped facilitate support activities within information technology. As each version of Sencha's products was released, Peter implemented new applications and built the company's first mobile app using Sencha Touch. His most compelling and highly-used application was a work review tool that combined big data technology with the power and flexibility of Sencha Ext JS and Sencha Charts.

> I would like to thank my wife, Jennifer, and my children, Jonathan, Lucas, Zachary, and Lilyanna, for their patience and understanding while I reviewed this book and went to class and work. It has been a long road to where we are, and their love and dedication is what keeps me moving every day. I would like to acknowledge my brothers, family, and friends, who are a constant encouragement in my life. Finally, I would like to thank God for blessing me with all He has, and for the strength when I didn't think there was any left.

Matt Goldspink is currently the lead engineer at Vlocity, Inc., based in San Francisco, working on their mobile and web platform. Prior to this, he held various roles at start-ups, banks, and also spent time as a technology trainer. Matt was the lead developer and architect for an award-winning mobile web platform for one of the world's leading investment banks. He has been a user of the Sencha framework for 5 years and was a speaker at their annual conference.

> I'd like to thank my partner, Mary, for supporting and encouraging me in all I do.

Shinobu Kawano is a JavaScript programmer based in Tokyo. Earlier, he was working for Canon IT Solutions Inc., as a solutions consultant of Sencha-featured system development. Currently, he is working as a sales engineer of Sencha-featured system development in the same company. His Twitter handle is `@kawanoshinobu`.

He has been addicted to Sencha frameworks since 2011, and he is the author of *Sencha Touch Perfect Guide – HTML5 mobile web application framework*, *ASCII MEDIA WORKS Inc.*, which was published in 2013 in Japanese.

Michael McCurrey is the software development manager for Ping Golf, a leader in the golf industry. His primary responsibility is designing and implementing solutions that use cutting-edge enterprise technologies to fit the company's varied needs across the globe. He has held a number of positions in the past, including software engineer, development team leader, and a C# trainer. Michael earned his bachelor's and master's degree from Ottawa University, and is currently pursuing a doctoral in information technology.

I would like to thank my wife, Sunni McCurrey, for her unwavering support while I used my personal time to review this book. I would also like to thank my children, Mickie, Zachary, and Daimon.

www.PacktPub.com

Support files, eBooks, discount offers, and more

For support files and downloads related to your book, please visit www.PacktPub.com.

Did you know that Packt offers eBook versions of every book published, with PDF and ePub files available? You can upgrade to the eBook version at www.PacktPub.com and as a print book customer, you are entitled to a discount on the eBook copy. Get in touch with us at service@packtpub.com for more details.

At www.PacktPub.com, you can also read a collection of free technical articles, sign up for a range of free newsletters and receive exclusive discounts and offers on Packt books and eBooks.

https://www2.packtpub.com/books/subscription/packtlib

Do you need instant solutions to your IT questions? PacktLib is Packt's online digital book library. Here, you can search, access, and read Packt's entire library of books.

Why subscribe?

- Fully searchable across every book published by Packt
- Copy and paste, print, and bookmark content
- On demand and accessible via a web browser

Free access for Packt account holders

If you have an account with Packt at www.PacktPub.com, you can use this to access PacktLib today and view 9 entirely free books. Simply use your login credentials for immediate access.

Table of Contents

Preface

Sencha Charts is a new and powerful library used to create rich and beautiful charts for your Sencha Touch and Ext JS applications. Built in HTML5, Sencha Charts is optimized for performance and fully supportive of gestures and touch devices to make visualizing data effortless.

What this book covers

Chapter 1, Fundamentals of Sencha Charts, covers the basic drawing constructs, such as line, circle, path, text, which are the fundamental building blocks of any charting library. It is using these drawing constructs that bar charts, pie charts, and so on, are created. This chapter explains how these building blocks are drawn on a screen using SVG and HTML5 Canvas APIs. It ends the discussion by showing how Sencha Charts uses these different APIs to abstract the device-specific and API-specific differences.

Chapter 2, Working with Out-of-the-box Charts, takes you through the different types of charts — cartesian, polar, and spacefilling — that come along with Sencha Charts, and demonstrates how they can be used in your application for data visualization. This chapter also offers the opportunity to understand the different concepts involved in creating charts using Sencha Charts, such as axis, legend, series, sprite, and so on.

Chapter 3, Sencha Charts Architecture, goes inside the framework and shows how the framework implements the architecture, internally. This chapter describes the overall architecture of Sencha Charts and sets the foundation for the subsequent topics where you will create custom charts.

Chapter 4, Creating a Custom Cartesian Chart, describes the detailed steps involved in creating a custom cartesian chart and provides the practical implementation of a stock chart — William %R — to apply the steps.

Chapter 5, Creating a Custom Polar Chart, describes the detailed steps involved in creating a custom polar chart and provides a practical implementation of a Market Clock to apply the steps.

Chapter 6, Creating a Custom Spacefilling Chart, describes the detailed steps involved in creating a custom spacefilling chart and provides the practical implementation of a periodic table to apply the steps.

Chapter 7, Theming, describes how theming — axis styling, legend styling, series colors, and so on — is supported in Sencha Charts and how you can leverage it to theme your charts. It also explains the theming-related considerations that you must have when you are implementing your own custom charts.

Chapter 8, Working with Touch Gestures, describes the different touch gestures that Sencha Charts supports and how some of the existing charts use them to engage users. It describes the configurations specific to different interactions and how to set them up on a chart. This chapter also explains how we can create custom interactions on a custom chart using touch gestures.

Chapter 9, Comparison with Other JavaScript Charting Libraries, compares Sencha Charts with other popular charting libraries, such as HighCharts, FusionCharts, amCharts, and Google Charts, to present a comparative study of different frameworks and their capabilities. It will describe, briefly, how the same task, for example, creating a custom cartesian chart, can be implemented in different libraries.

What you need for this book

You will need Sencha Cmd 5.0.2.270+, Ruby 2.0, Compass 1.0.1+, Oracle JDK 1.7+, Chrome browser (latest), a web server — XAMPP v3.2.1+ with Apache and a Windows, Linux, or Mac OS.

Who this book is for

This book is for Ext JS or Sencha Touch developer, designer, or architect who wants to build enterprise-scale data visualization capabilities using Sencha.

Conventions

In this book, you will find a number of text styles that distinguish between different kinds of information. Here are some examples of these styles and an explanation of their meaning.

Code words in text, database table names, folder names, filenames, file extensions, pathnames, dummy URLs, user input, and Twitter handles are shown as follows: "The `for` loop iterates through each of the sprites — sectors — that were created and sets their `startRho` and `endRho` attributes based on the runtime calculation."

A block of code is set as follows:

```
//show cross-hair
var overlay = drawCt.getSurface('overlay');
var hl, vl, headerOffset;

hl = this.createLine(-x0, -y0, -x0, -y0);
vl = this.createLine(-x0, -y0, -x0, -y0);
hl.lineDash = [5,5];
vl.lineDash = [5,5];
hl = overlay.add(hl);
```

When we wish to draw your attention to a particular part of a code block, the relevant lines or items are set in bold:

```
items: [{
    xtype: 'periodictable',
    interactions: ['sce-itemhighlight'],
...

listeners: {
    itemhighlight: function(itemSelected) {
        if (itemSelected && itemSelected.record) {
            alert('Selected element is: ' +
                itemSelected.record.get(itemSelected.field));
        }
    }
}
```

Any command-line input or output is written as follows:

```
sencha generate app SCE /path/to/application/folder
```

New terms and **important words** are shown in bold. Words that you see on the screen, for example, in menus or dialog boxes, appear in the text like this: "There are two ways to draw in a browser—**Scalable Vector Graphics (SVG)** and **Canvas API.**"

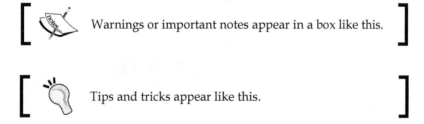

[Warnings or important notes appear in a box like this.]

[Tips and tricks appear like this.]

Reader feedback

Feedback from our readers is always welcome. Let us know what you think about this book—what you liked or disliked. Reader feedback is important for us as it helps us develop titles that you will really get the most out of.

To send us general feedback, simply e-mail feedback@packtpub.com, and mention the book's title in the subject of your message.

If there is a topic that you have expertise in and you are interested in either writing or contributing to a book, see our author guide at www.packtpub.com/authors.

Customer support

Now that you are the proud owner of a Packt book, we have a number of things to help you to get the most from your purchase.

Downloading the example code

You can download the example code files from your account at http://www.packtpub.com for all the Packt Publishing books you have purchased. If you purchased this book elsewhere, you can visit http://www.packtpub.com/support and register to have the files e-mailed directly to you.

Downloading the color images of this book

We also provide you with a PDF file that has color images of the screenshots/ diagrams used in this book. The color images will help you better understand the changes in the output. You can download this file from https://www.packtpub.com/sites/default/files/downloads/9767OS_ColorImage.pdf.

Errata

Although we have taken every care to ensure the accuracy of our content, mistakes do happen. If you find a mistake in one of our books—maybe a mistake in the text or the code—we would be grateful if you could report this to us. By doing so, you can save other readers from frustration and help us improve subsequent versions of this book. If you find any errata, please report them by visiting http://www.packtpub.com/submit-errata, selecting your book, clicking on the **Errata Submission Form** link, and entering the details of your errata. Once your errata are verified, your submission will be accepted and the errata will be uploaded to our website or added to any list of existing errata under the Errata section of that title.

To view the previously submitted errata, go to `https://www.packtpub.com/books/content/support` and enter the name of the book in the search field. The required information will appear under the **Errata** section.

Piracy

Piracy of copyrighted material on the Internet is an ongoing problem across all media. At Packt, we take the protection of our copyright and licenses very seriously. If you come across any illegal copies of our works in any form on the Internet, please provide us with the location address or website name immediately so that we can pursue a remedy.

Please contact us at `copyright@packtpub.com` with a link to the suspected pirated material.

We appreciate your help in protecting our authors and our ability to bring you valuable content.

Questions

If you have a problem with any aspect of this book, you can contact us at `questions@packtpub.com`, and we will do our best to address the problem.

1
Fundamentals of Sencha Charts

Data visualization has always been an integral part of an application, because of its power to quickly disseminate information. It is no different for an application developed using Sencha Ext JS or Sencha Touch frameworks. Recently, with the launch of Ext JS 5, Sencha has created a separate charting package—Sencha Charts—to add charting capability to an application. The beauty is that the same Sencha Charts library works inside desktop applications that run Ext JS, as well as in touch- or mobile-based applications that run Sencha Touch.

There are two ways to draw in a browser—**Scalable Vector Graphics (SVG)** and **Canvas API**. Though VML also exists for older IE browsers, we have excluded it for brevity. All the JavaScript charting libraries use SVG and Canvas API to offer charting capability to their users—for rendering as well as interactions. Understanding them will provide the foundation that is needed to understand Sencha Charts and its capabilities, and more importantly, reasons to use it.

SVG and Canvas are supported by browsers to render graphics. SVG was introduced in 1999 to render vector graphics, which can scale up or down, based on the screen resolution, without any visual distortion, as compared to raster one. SVG works similar to XML where you work with elements, attributes, and styles. SVG is a retained mode graphics model that is persisted in browser memory and we can manipulate it through code. This manipulation leads to automatic re-rendering where the user sees the updated drawing.

Canvas was a new specification brought to us by Apple in 2004. It follows an immediate mode graphics model, where it renders the drawing and forgets it. It does not have a built-in scene graph that SVG has, where it retains the graphics in memory and allows its manipulation. So, to recreate the same drawing, you will have to call the APIs to redraw it on the canvas.

In this chapter, we will do the following:

- Create a chart using SVG
- Create a chart using the HTML5 Canvas API
- Create a chart using the Sencha Charts API
- Compare the three to understand the advantages of using Sencha Charts

Introducing the sample chart

For demonstration and comparison, we will create a chart using Canvas API and SVG, and then we will create the same using Sencha Charts APIs.

Our sample chart, as shown in the following figure, will have:

- x (horizontal) and y (vertical) axes with labels
- A column chart with circular markers in the middle of each bar
- An area chart
- A crosshair that appears on mousemove

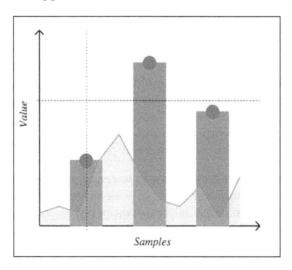

In our implementation, we will use a few terms, coordinates, and calculations. They are highlighted in the following diagram:

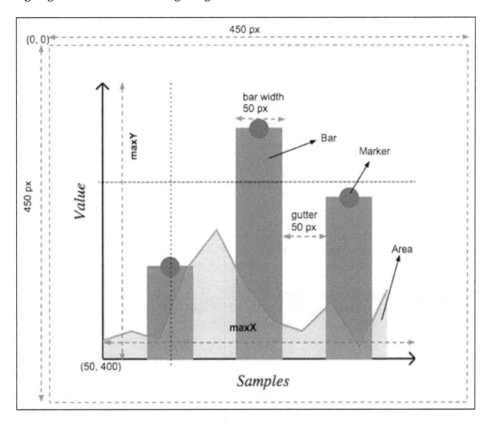

Canvas and SVG

In this section, we will see how we can create the sample chart, described earlier, using Canvas API and SVG. Each of these technologies has their own advantages and context in which they will be used. Their discussion is not in the scope of this book. You may refer to the W3 specifications for their detailed documentation.

Preparation

First of all, let's prepare our HTML to draw the chart. The Canvas APIs work with the `<canvas>` element, whereas SVG APIs work with the `<svg>` element.

The following table shows the HTML page for Canvas-based and SVG-based drawing approaches. The `ch01_01.html` code, which is on the left-hand side, contains the implementation using Canvas APIs, whereas `ch01_02.html` contains the implementation based on SVG APIs.

ch01_01.html	ch01_02.html

``html
<!DOCTYPE HTML>
<html>
    <head>
    </head>
<body>
<canvas id="my-canvas" width="450"
height="450" style="position:
absolute; left: 0; top: 0; z-index:
1;"></canvas>
<canvas id="overlay" width="450"
height="450" style="position:
absolute; left: 0; top: 0; z-index:
2;"></canvas>
 	
<script>
    //code will go here
</script>
</body>
</html>
``
	``html
	<!DOCTYPE html>
	<html>
	    <head>
	    </head>
	<body>
	<svg id="my-drawing"
	width="450" height="450"
	xmlns="http://www.
	w3.org/2000/svg"
	    xmlns:xlink="http://
	www.w3.org/1999/xlink"></svg>
	
	<script>
	    //code will go here
	</script>
	</body>
	
	</html>
	``

All the JavaScript code that we will be writing will go inside the `<script>` tag.

Let's start by creating some helper methods for our chart, which we will use later to create the actual chart. We will have the Canvas and SVG code side by side for easier comparison.

Creating a line

To create a line, Canvas provides path APIs — moveTo and lineTo — whereas SVG provides the <line> element. The following screenshot shows the code to create a line, which we will use to create the chart axis, and crosshair lines:

ch01_01.html	ch01_02.html

``
<script>
  function createLine(ctx, x1,
y1, x2, y2, sw) {
    ctx.beginPath();
    ctx.moveTo(x1, y1);
    ctx.lineTo(x2, y2);
    ctx.lineWidth = sw ? sw : 2;
    ctx.strokeStyle = 'black';
    ctx.stroke();
    ctx.closePath();
  }
``
	``
	<script>
	  var NS = "http://www.
	w3.org/2000/svg";
	  function createLine(x1, y1, x2,
	y2, sw) {
	    var line = document.
	createElementNS(NS, 'line');
	    line.setAttribute('x1', x1);
	    line.setAttribute('y1', y1);
	    line.setAttribute('x2', x2);
	    line.setAttribute('y2', y2);
	    line.style.stroke = 'black';
	    line.style["stroke-width"] =
	sw ? sw : 2;
	
	    return line;
	  }
	``

Creating an axis

An axis is a combination of a line and an arrow head. In the following code, the createAxis method can create an axis and the arrow head based on the line coordinates and the axis direction value, which will be "v" to indicate vertical axis; or "h" to indicate horizontal axis. The direction value is used to calculate the path for drawing the arrow head.

In the following table, the code in the first column shows the implementation using the Canvas API, whereas the code in the second column shows the SVG equivalent of it:

ch01_01.html	ch01_02.html

```
    function
createAxis(ctx, x1, y1,
x2, y2, direction) {
    createLine(ctx, x1,
y1, x2, y2);

    //draw arrow head
    if (direction ===
"v") {
        ctx.beginPath();
        ctx.moveTo(x1, y2);
        ctx.lineTo(x1 -
10*Math.sin(Math.PI/4),
y2 + 10*Math.cos(Math.
PI/4));
        ctx.moveTo(x1, y2);
        ctx.lineTo(x1 +
10*Math.sin(Math.PI/4),
y2 + 10*Math.cos(Math.
PI/4));
        ctx.lineWidth = 2,
        ctx.strokeStyle =
'black',
        ctx.stroke();
        ctx.closePath();
    }

    if (direction ===
"h") {
        ctx.beginPath();
        ctx.moveTo(x2, y1);
        ctx.lineTo(x2 -
10*Math.cos(Math.PI/4),
x2 - 10*Math.sin(Math.
PI/4));
        ctx.moveTo(x2, y1);
        ctx.lineTo(x2 -
10*Math.cos(Math.PI/4),
x2 + 10*Math.sin(Math.
PI/4));
        ctx.lineWidth = 2;
        ctx.strokeStyle =
'black';
        ctx.stroke();
        ctx.closePath();
    }
}
```

```
  function createPath(p, stroke, fill) {
    var path = document.createElementNS(NS,
'path');

    path.setAttribute('d', p);
    path.style.stroke = stroke ? stroke :
'black';
    path.style["stroke-width"] = 2;
    path.style.fill = fill ? fill : 'none'


    return path;
  }

  function createAxis(x1, y1, x2, y2, direction)
{
    var axis = document.createElementNS(NS, 'g');

    var line = createLine(x1, y1, x2, y2);
    var ah;

    //draw arrow head
    if (direction === "v") {
      var p = 'M' + x1 + ',' + y2 + ' L' + (x1 -
10*Math.sin(Math.PI/4)) + ',' + (maxY + 10*Math.
cos(Math.PI/4));
        p += ' M' + x1 + ',' + y2 + ' L' + (x1 +
10*Math.sin(Math.PI/4)) + ',' + (maxY + 10*Math.
cos(Math.PI/4));
      ah = createPath(p);
    }

    if (direction === "h") {
      var p = 'M' + x2 + ',' + y1 + ' L' + (x2
- 10*Math.cos(Math.PI/4)) + ',' + (x2 - 10*Math.
sin(Math.PI/4));
        p += ' M' + x2 + ',' + y1 + ' L' + (x2 -
10*Math.cos(Math.PI/4)) + ',' + (x2 + 10*Math.
sin(Math.PI/4));
      ah = createPath(p);
    }

    axis.appendChild(line);
    axis.appendChild(ah);

    return axis;
  }
```

Creating an axis label

The createLabel method creates a text label for an axis based on the specified direction. The Canvas approach uses transformation — translate and rotate — to render the vertical label, whereas the SVG approach uses the writing-mode style attribute of the <text> element. You may also use <tspan> with transformations to show the vertical axis label.

In the following table, the code in the first column shows the implementation of the method using the Canvas API, whereas the code in the second column shows the equivalent implementation using SVG specification:

ch01_01.html	ch01_02.html
| ```
function createLabel(ctx, x,
y, txt, direction) {

    ctx.font = 'Italic 1.1em
Aerial';

    if (direction === 'v') {
        ctx.translate(x, y);
        ctx.rotate(-Math.PI/2);
        ctx.fillText(txt, 0, 0);

        //reset transformation
        ctx.setTransform(1, 0, 0,
1, 0, 0);
    } else {
        ctx.fillText(txt, x, y);
    }
}
``` | ```
function createLabel(x, y, txt,
direction) {
    var text = document.
createElementNS(NS, 'text');

    text.setAttribute('x', x);
    text.setAttribute('y', y);
    text.style.font = 'Italic
1.1em Aerial';
    if (direction === 'v') {
        text.style['writing-mode']
= 'tb';
    }

    var node = document.
createTextNode(txt);
    text.appendChild(node);

    return text;
}
``` |

Creating a bar

To create a bar for our column chart, the `createBar` method draws a rectangle using the `rect` API of Canvas and the `<rect>` element of SVG.

ch01_01.html	ch01_02.html
```function createBar(ctx, x, y, w, h) { ctx.beginPath(); ctx.moveTo(x, y); ctx.rect(x, y, w, h); ctx.fillStyle = '#E13987'; ctx.lineWidth = 2; ctx.strokeStyle = '#E13987'; ctx.stroke(); ctx.fill(); ctx.closePath(); }```	```function createBar(x, y, w, h) { var rect = document.createElementNS(NS, 'rect'); rect.setAttribute('x', x); rect.setAttribute('y', y); rect.setAttribute('width', w); rect.setAttribute('height', h); rect.style.fill = '#E13987'; rect.style.stroke = '#E13987'; rect.style['stroke-width'] = 2; return rect; }```

Creating a marker on the bar

In our chart, we want to show circular markers on the top of the bars. The `createMarker` method will help us add markers to our drawing based on the location of its center and radius.

ch01_01.html	ch01_02.html
```function createMarker(ctx, cx, cy, r) { ctx.beginPath(); ctx.arc(cx, cy, r, 0, 2*Math.PI, false); ctx.fillStyle = '#6F5092'; ctx.lineWidth = 2; ctx.strokeStyle = '#6F5092'; ctx.stroke(); ctx.fill(); ctx.closePath(); }```	```function createMarker(cx, cy, r) { var circle = document.createElementNS(NS, 'circle'); circle.setAttribute('cx', cx); circle.setAttribute('cy', cy); circle.setAttribute('r', r); circle.style.fill = '#6F5092'; circle.style.stroke = '#6F5092'; circle.style['stroke-width'] = 2; return circle; }```

This ends the list of helper methods that we need to create our chart. Let's see how we can use them to create the final output.

Creating a chart

Now, we will enhance our script to create the chart in a step-by-step approach. We will start with the axis.

Axes

Before we start, we first need access to our drawing surface, either the `canvas` or `<svg>` element. Since we have already set the ID on the element, we can use the `document.getElementById` method to access them. Canvas API, however, requires us to additionally get the drawing context and use it for the drawing.

Once we have access to the drawing surface, we use the `createAxis` method to create the *x* and *y* axes, as shown in the following table:

ch01_01.html	ch01_02.html
| ```
    var canvas = document.
getElementById('my-canvas');
    var ctx = canvas.
getContext('2d');

    var samples = [100, 250, 175],
        gutter = 50,
        barWidth = 50,
        x0 = 50,
        y0 = 400,
        markerRadius = 10;


    //draw axes
    var maxX = x0 + samples.
length*(barWidth + gutter) +
gutter;
    var maxY = y0 - 250 - 50;
    createAxis(ctx, x0, y0, maxX,
y0, 'h');
    createAxis(ctx, x0, y0, x0,
maxY, 'v');
``` | ```
    var svg = document.
getElementById('my-drawing');

    var samples = [100, 250,
175],
        gutter = 50,
        barWidth = 50,
        x0 = 50,
        y0 = 400,
        markerRadius = 10;

    //draw axes
    var maxX = x0 + samples.
length*(barWidth + gutter) +
gutter;
    var maxY = y0 - 250 - 50;
    var xAxis = createAxis(x0,
y0, maxX, y0, 'h');
    var yAxis = createAxis(x0,
y0, x0, maxY, 'v');

    svg.appendChild(xAxis);
    svg.appendChild(yAxis);
``` |

The following screenshot shows the output with x and y axes. Each axis has an arrowhead as well:

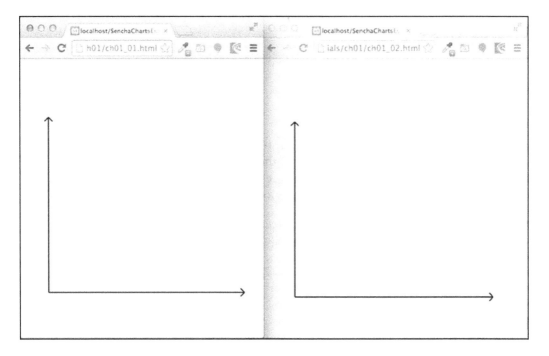

Axis label

To draw a label on an axis, use the `createLabel` method, as shown in the following table:

ch01_01.html	ch01_02.html
```//create axis label createLabel(ctx, maxX/2, y0 + 30, 'Samples'); createLabel(ctx, x0 - 20, y0 - (y0 - maxY)/2, 'Value', 'v');```	```//create axis label var xLabel = createLabel(maxX/2, y0 + 30, 'Samples'); var yLabel = createLabel(x0 - 20, y0 - (y0 - maxY)/2, 'Value', 'v'); svg.appendChild(xLabel); svg.appendChild(yLabel);```

The following output is produced to show the axis label:

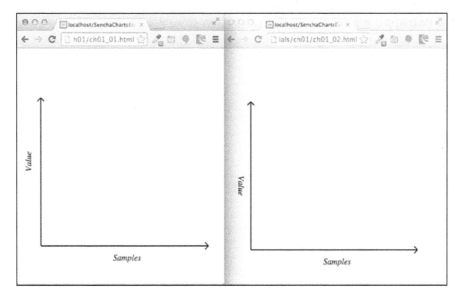

Bar chart with a marker

To create the bar for each sample data, we will use the `createBar` method and `createMarker` to show the marker on the top of each bar, as shown in the following table:

ch01_01.html	ch01_02.html
``//draw bars
  for (var i=0; i<samples.
length; i++) {
    var x, y, w = barWidth, h =
samples[i];
    x = x0 + gutter + i*(w +
gutter);
    y = y0 - h;

    createBar(ctx, x, y, w, h);
    createMarker(ctx, x + w/2,
y, markerRadius);
  }``` | ```//draw bars
  for (var i=0; i<samples.length;
i++) {
    var x, y, w = barWidth, h =
samples[i];
    x = x0 + gutter + i*(w +
gutter);
    y = y0 - h;

    var bar = createBar(x, y, w,
h);
    var marker = createMarker(x
+ w/2, y, markerRadius);

    svg.appendChild(bar);
    svg.appendChild(marker);

  }``` |

You may refer to the second figure in the *Introducing the sample chart* section for the `barWidth` and `gutter` values. The following screenshot shows the output produced from the two applications:

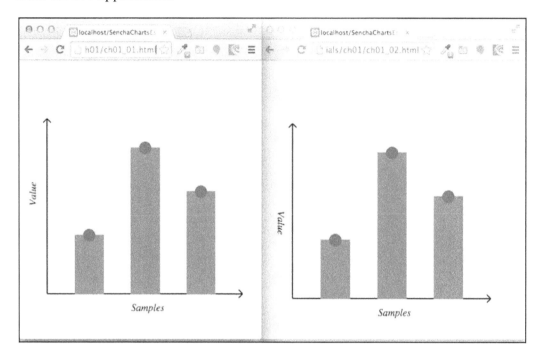

Creating an area chart with line stroking

Our next step is to create an area chart. First, we will show the line and then we will fill the area.

The following code shows how to create the area chart with line stroke using a different sample—`areaSamples`:

ch01_01.html	ch01_02.html
``//draw area chart
var areaSamples = [20, 30, 20,
100, 140, 80, 40, 30, 60, 10, 75];
var n = areaSamples.length;
var d = (maxX - x0)/n;
//distance between the points
var start = true;
for (var i=0; i<n; i++) {
  var x = x0 + i*d , y = y0 -
areaSamples[i];

    if (start) {
      ctx.beginPath();
      ctx.moveTo(x, y);
      start = false;
    }
    ctx.lineTo(x, y);
  }
  ctx.lineWidth = 2,
  ctx.strokeStyle = '#00904B',
  ctx.stroke();
  ctx.closePath();``` | ```//draw area chart
var areaSamples = [20, 30,
20, 100, 140, 80, 40, 30, 60,
10, 75];
var n = areaSamples.length;
var d = (maxX - x0)/n;
//distance between the points
var start = true;
var p = '';
for (var i=0; i<n; i++) {
  var x = x0 + i*d , y = y0 -
areaSamples[i];

    if (start) {
      p += 'M' + x + ',' + y;
      start = false;
    }

    p += ' L' + x + ',' + y;
  }

  //area - with border
  var area = createPath(p,
'#00904B');
  svg.appendChild(area);``` |

We have used path APIs to create the line chart, which we will fill in the next section to make it an area chart. Run the two codes and you will see the following output:

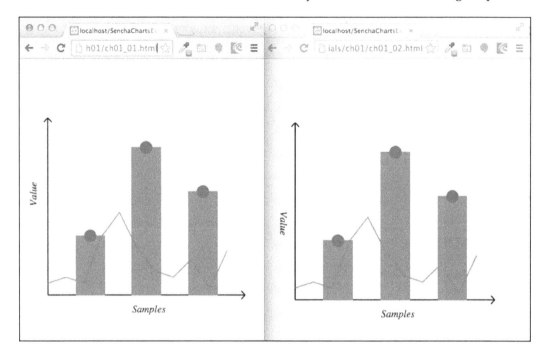

Creating an area chart with fill

Now, let's fill the area under the line chart that we drew earlier to make it an area chart. To fill the area, we will have to end the path at its starting point.

Since we have added the area chart after the bar, the bar would be hidden behind the area chart. So, we will set the transparency when we fill the area. This way, the user can see the bar behind the area. To set the transparency in Canvas, we set the `globalAlpha` parameter, whereas in SVG, it is a bit more involved. We have to create a `mask` element with transparency level and use it to fill the area.

In the following table, the code in the first column shows the implementation using the Canvas API, whereas, the code in the second column shows the corresponding implementation using SVG:

ch01_01.html	ch01_02.html

``
//fill the area chart
start = true;
ctx.globalAlpha = 0.5;
ctx.fillStyle = '#64BD4F';
for (var i=0; i<n; i++) {
    var x = x0 + i*d , y = y0 -
areaSamples[i];
 	
    if (start) {
        ctx.beginPath();
        ctx.moveTo(x, y0);
        start = false;
    }
    ctx.lineTo(x, y);
 	
    if (i === (n - 1)) {
        ctx.lineTo(x, y0);
    }
}
ctx.fill();
ctx.closePath();
``
	``
	//fill the area chart
	    p += ' L' + x + ',' + y0 + ' L'
	+ x0 + ',' + y0 + ' Z';
	    var fillArea = createPath(p,
	'none', '#64BD4F');
	
	    //transparency for the fill
	area
	    var defs = document.
	createElementNS(NS, 'defs');
	    var mask = document.
	createElementNS(NS, 'mask');
	    mask.setAttribute('id',
	'areamask');
	    mask.setAttribute('x', 0);
	    mask.setAttribute('y', 0);
	    mask.setAttribute('width',
	450);
	    mask.setAttribute('height',
	450);
	    var fillArea1 = document.
	createElementNS(NS, 'path');
	    fillArea1.setAttribute('d', p);
	    fillArea1.style.fill =
	'#666666';
	    mask.appendChild(fillArea1);
	    defs.appendChild(mask);
	    svg.appendChild(defs);
	
	    fillArea.style.fill =
	'#64BD4F';
	    fillArea.setAttribute('mask',
	'url(#areamask)');
	    svg.appendChild(fillArea);
	``

The following screenshot shows the output produced by these two codes:

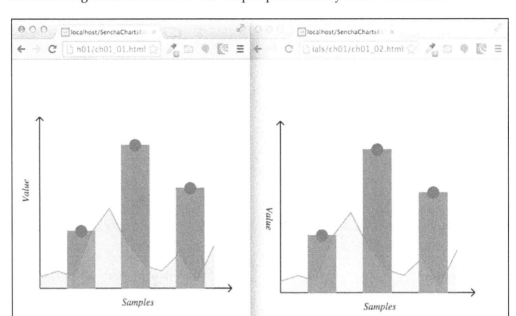

Crosshair lines

The last item we are left with is crosshair lines. To show the crosshair line on mousemove in the Canvas approach, we will add one more <canvas> element on top (that is, higher z-index) of the existing one as an overlay layer. It is this overlay canvas that we will use to render crosshair lines. Here is the code snippet showing an additional overlay <canvas> element added to the document body:

```
<body>
    <canvas id="my-canvas" width="450" height="450" style="position:
absolute; left: 0; top: 0; z-index: 1;"></canvas>
    <canvas id="overlay" width="450" height="450" style="position:
absolute; left: 0; top: 0; z-index: 2;"></canvas>
<script>
...
```

We register the handler for mousemove on the overlay canvas. The handler clears the canvas using the clearRect API so that old lines get cleared before adding the crosshair lines.

In the SVG approach, we will use the same <svg> element. The lines are added beforehand and the handler code moves them to the new location based on mouse position by setting their coordinate related attributes.

There is a check we can make to ensure that we don't show the crosshair if the mouse is outside of the chart area.

The following table shows the code related to crosshair for Canvas as well as SVG:

ch01_01.html	ch01_02.html

``javascript
    //show cross-hair
    var overlay = document.
getElementById('overlay');
    var overCtx = overlay.
getContext('2d');
 	
    var lineDash = overCtx.
getLineDash();
    overCtx.setLineDash([5,5]);
    overlay.
addEventListener('mousemove',
function(evt) {
      overCtx.clearRect(0, 0,
overlay.width, overlay.height);
      var rect = overlay.
getBoundingClientRect();
      var x = evt.clientX - rect.
left,
      y = evt.clientY - rect.top;
      //don't show the cross-hair
if we are outside the chart area
      if (x < x0 || x > maxX || y
< maxY || y > y0) {
        return;
      }
 	
      overCtx.beginPath();
      overCtx.moveTo(x0 - 5, y);
      overCtx.lineTo(maxX, y);
      overCtx.moveTo(x, maxY);
      overCtx.lineTo(x, y0 + 10);
      overCtx.strokeStyle =
'black',
      overCtx.stroke();
      overCtx.closePath();
    }, false);
``
	``javascript
	    //show cross-hair
	      var hl = createLine(-x0,
	-y0, -maxX, -y0);
	      var vl = createLine(-x0,
	-y0, -x0, -maxY);
	      hl.style['stroke-dasharray']
	= [5,5];
	      vl.style['stroke-dasharray']
	= [5,5];
	      svg.appendChild(hl);
	      svg.appendChild(vl);
	      svg.
	addEventListener('mousemove',
	function(evt) {
	      var x = evt.offsetX || evt.
	clientX,
	      y = evt.offsetY || evt.
	clientY;
	      //don't show the cross-hair
	if we are outside the chart area
	      if (x < x0 || x > maxX || y
	< maxY || y > y0) {
	        return;
	      }
	
	      hl.setAttribute('x1', x0 -
	5);
	      hl.setAttribute('y1', y);
	      hl.setAttribute('x2', maxX);
	      hl.setAttribute('y2', y);
	
	      vl.setAttribute('x1', x);
	      vl.setAttribute('y1', maxY);
	      vl.setAttribute('x2', x);
	      vl.setAttribute('y2', y0 +
	10);
	
	    });
	``

Here is the output of the two codes showing the crosshair lines when a user moves the mouse in the chart area:

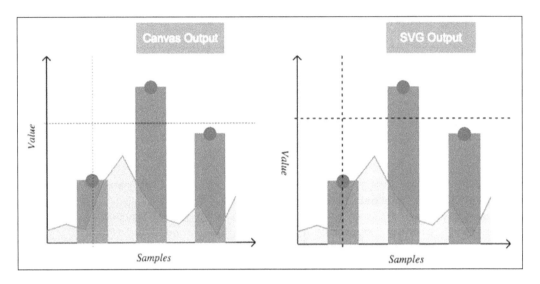

So, we have our final output. Great! But wait! Imagine that you are a charts library developer or someone who wants to add charting capability to your application and has to support different browsers; some of them support SVG (for example, older ones), whereas some of them support Canvas. You can visit `http://caniuse.com/` to review specific browser-related support. To ensure that your charts render on both types of browser, you will have to implement your code in SVG as well as Canvas, and then, based on the browser support, your code has to use one of them. The problem becomes even bigger if you have to support old IE browsers that support VML, as the APIs and approaches differ.

This is exactly the kind of problem we can solve using an abstraction called **Surface**, which is offered by Sencha Charts. Let's look at the Surface abstraction, what mechanism it offers for drawing, and how we can use them to create the same chart that we have created using the SVG and Canvas APIs.

Sencha Charts Surface API

Sencha Charts offers complete charting capability with built-in charts to serve your data visualization needs. While we will look at the different out-of-box charts and their extensions in subsequent chapters, here we will look at their abstraction class—`Ext.draw.Surface`—which abstracts the underlying API differences across browsers and provides a single consistent API, which renders drawings on SVG, Canvas, or VML based on what the underlying browser supports. The following diagram depicts the `Surface` class that translates its APIs to the underlying VML, SVG, or Canvas APIs based on the browser support:

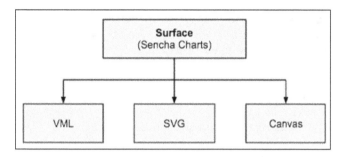

To demonstrate the Surface API and its benefits, let's create a project using **Sencha Cmd** by running the following command:

```
sencha generate app SCE /path/to/application/folder
```

Modify your `app.json` file to add Sencha Charts support to your project by adding `sencha-charts` to the `requires` config. After this, refresh the application by running the following command so that Sencha Charts package is included into the application:

```
sencha app refresh
```

Axes

Sencha Cmd will generate a `Main` view class inside the `app/view/main` folder, which is the initial view rendered on the screen. Replace the content of the file with the following code to show the axes:

```
Ext.define('SCE.view.main.Main', {
    extend: 'Ext.container.Container',

    xtype: 'app-main',

    height: 850,
```

```
        width: 850,

        items: [{
            xtype: 'draw',
            title: 'Chart',
            height: 500,
            width: 500
        }],

        createLine: function(x1, y1, x2, y2, sw) {
            return {
                type: 'path',
                stroke: 'black',
                path: 'M' + x1 + ',' + y1 + ' L' + x2 + ',' + y2,
                lineWidth: sw ? sw : 2
            };

        },

        createPath: function(p, stroke, fill, opacity) {
            return {
                type: 'path',
                path: p,
                stroke: stroke ? stroke : 'black',
                lineWidth: 2,
                fillStyle: fill ? fill : 'none',
                fillOpacity: opacity ? opacity : 1
            };
        },

        createAxis: function(x1, y1, x2, y2, direction) {
            var line = this.createLine(x1, y1, x2, y2);
            var ah;

            //draw arrow head
            if (direction === "v") {
                var p = 'M' + x1 + ',' + y2 + ' L' + (x1 - 10*Math.
sin(Math.PI/4)) + ',' + (this.maxY + 10*Math.cos(Math.PI/4));
                p += ' M' + x1 + ',' + y2 + ' L' + (x1 + 10*Math.sin(Math.
PI/4)) + ',' + (this.maxY + 10*Math.cos(Math.PI/4));

                ah = this.createPath(p);
            }

            if (direction === "h") {
                var p = 'M' + x2 + ',' + y1 + ' L' + (this.maxX - 10*Math.
cos(Math.PI/4)) + ',' + (this.maxX - 10*Math.sin(Math.PI/4));
```

```
            p += ' M' + x2 + ',' + y1 + ' L' + (this.maxX - 10*Math.
    cos(Math.PI/4)) + ',' + (this.maxX + 10*Math.sin(Math.PI/4));

            ah = this.createPath(p);
        }

        var axis = Ext.create('Ext.draw.sprite.Composite', {});
        axis.add(line);
        axis.add(ah);

        return axis;
    },

    afterRender: function() {
        var samples = [100, 250, 175],
            gutter = 50,
            barWidth = 50,
            x0 = 50,
            y0 = 400,
            markerRadius = 10;

        var drawCt = this.down('draw');

        var surface = drawCt.getSurface();

    //draw axes
    this.maxX = x0 + samples.length*(barWidth + gutter) + gutter;
    this.maxY = y0 - 250 - 50;
    surface.add(this.createAxis(x0, y0, this.maxX, y0, 'h'));
    surface.add(this.createAxis(x0, y0, x0, this.maxY, 'v'));

    this.callParent(arguments);
    }
}));
```

The preceding code creates a container with a container with a draw component that shows the *x* and *y* axes. The draw component contains the surface object that offers drawing APIs.

The createLine method creates a line using the path sprite. The createPath method creates a path using the path sprite. This is used to create the arrowhead of the axis.

The following code snippet creates two axes and adds them to the surface. The Surface class internally and uses VML/SVG/Canvas APIs to render the drawing on the screen:

```
surface.add(this.createAxis(x0, y0, this.maxX, y0, 'h'));
surface.add(this.createAxis(x0, y0, x0, this.maxY, 'v'));
```

The following screenshot shows the output produced by the preceding code:

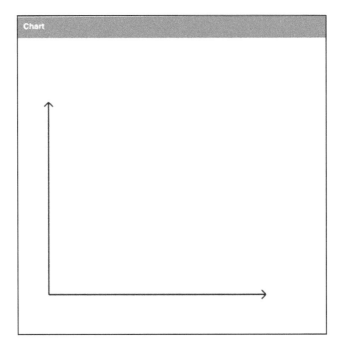

Axis label, bars, and markers

Let's add a member method to the `SCE.view.main.Main` class to create the axis label. The following method uses the `text` sprite to create a label:

```
createLabel: function(x, y, txt) {

    return {
        type: 'text',
        x: x,
        y: y,
        text: txt,
        font: '1.1em arial italic'
    };

}
```

The `createBar` member method uses a rectangle sprite to create a bar for our bar chart.

```
createBar: function(x, y, w, h) {
    return {
        type: 'rect',
```

```
            x: x,
            y: y,
            width: w,
            height: h,
            fillStyle: '#E13987',
            stroke: '#E13987',
            lineWidth: 2
        };
    }
```

The following member method creates a marker at the specified coordinate:

```
    createMarker: function(cx, cy, r) {
        return {
            type: 'circle',
            cx: cx,
            cy: cy,
            r: r,
            fillStyle: '#6F5092',
            stroke: '#6F5092',
            lineWidth: 2
        };
    }
```

Now, let's add the following code to the `afterRender` method, before the `this.callParent()` call, to draw the axis label and bars with markers:

```
//create axis label
var xLabel = this.createLabel(this.maxX/2, y0 + 30, 'Samples');
var yLabel = this.createLabel(x0 - 40, y0 - (y0 - this.maxY)/2,
'Value');
yLabel.rotationRads = -Math.PI/2;

surface.add(xLabel);
surface.add(yLabel);

//draw bars
for (var i=0; i<samples.length; i++) {
    var x, y, w = barWidth, h = samples[i];
    x = x0 + gutter + i*(w + gutter);
    y = y0 - h;

    var bar = this.createBar(x, y, w, h);
    var marker = this.createMarker(x + w/2, y, markerRadius);

    surface.add(bar);
    surface.add(marker);

}
```

Refreshing the URL in the browser, the code will produce the following output:

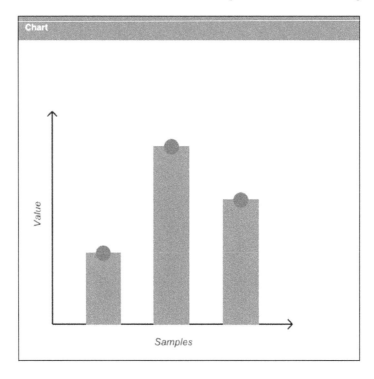

Area chart

To create the area chart, add the following code to the `afterRender` member method before the `this.callParent()` call:

```
//draw area chart
var areaSamples = [20, 30, 20, 100, 140, 80, 40, 30, 60, 10, 75];
var n = areaSamples.length;
var gutter = (this.maxX - x0)/n;
var start = true;
var p = '';
for (var i=0; i<n; i++) {
    var x = x0 + i*gutter , y = y0 - areaSamples[i];

    if (start) {
        p += 'M' + x + ',' + y;
        start = false;
    }
}
```

```
    p += ' L' + x + ',' + y;
}

//area - with border
var area = this.createPath(p, '#00904B');
surface.add(area);

//fill the area chart
p += ' L' + x + ',' + y0 + ' L' + x0 + ',' + y0 + ' Z';
var fillArea = this.createPath(p,'none','#64BD4F', 0.5);
surface.add(fillArea);
```

The following screenshot shows the output produced after the preceding code is added:

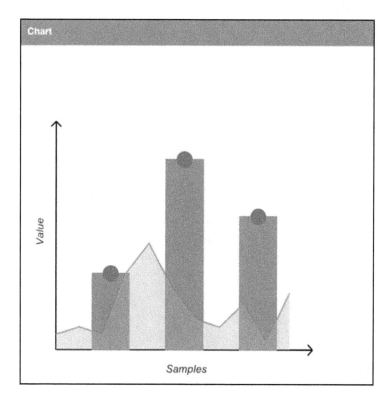

Creating the crosshair

The last item is creating the crosshair. The following code adds two lines to the overlay surface and then the mousemove handler changes its position by setting its path attributes:

```
//show cross-hair
var overlay = drawCt.getSurface('overlay');
var hl, vl, headerOffset;

hl = this.createLine(-x0, -y0, -x0, -y0);
vl = this.createLine(-x0, -y0, -x0, -y0);
hl.lineDash = [5,5];
vl.lineDash = [5,5];
hl = overlay.add(hl);
vl = overlay.add(vl);
this.getEl().addListener('mousemove', function(evt, target) {
    var x = evt.getX(),
        y = evt.getY();

    //don't show the cross-hair if we are outside the chart area
    if (x < x0 || x > this.maxX || y < this.maxY || y > y0) {
        return;
    }

    headerOffset = drawCt.getHeader().getHeight();

    hl.setAttributes({
        path: 'M' + (x0 - 5) + ',' + (y - headerOffset) + ' L' + this.
maxX + ',' + (y - headerOffset)
    });

    vl.setAttributes({
        path: 'M' + x + ',' + this.maxY + ' L' + x + ',' + (y0 + 10)
    });

    overlay.renderFrame();
}, this);
```

The overlay surface sits on top of the main surface that we used earlier to draw the axes, bar, area chart, and so on. We will discuss in more detail the different types of surfaces when we get to *Chapter 3, Sencha Charts Architecture*.

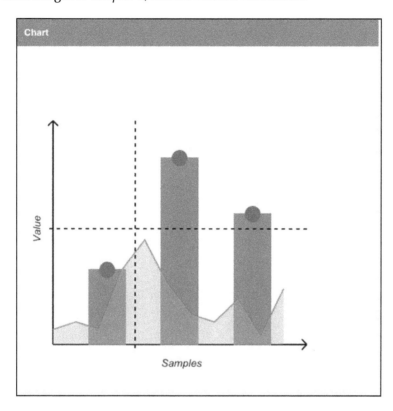

Summary

In this chapter, we reviewed the supported browser drawing formats—Canvas and SVG—to create a drawing and we used them to create a basic chart. These are basic building blocks of any JavaScript charting library, such as Sencha Charts, FusionCharts, HighCharts, amCharts, and so on. In the second half of the chapter, we looked at the issues that these different APIs present when it comes to creating charts that work on different browsers and platforms, and how we can use the Surface APIs of Sencha Charts to address them. In the subsequent chapters, we will build on top of these fundamentals to understand more about Sencha Charts.

2
Working with Out-of-the-box Charts

In the previous chapter, we saw how one can create a chart using the Sencha Charts Surface API. The only issue is that Surface is still a very low-level API providing drawing primitives, which can be used to create any drawing, including charts. We will have to write a lot of code to create a chart using these drawing primitives, handling events, resizing charts, data binding, theming, and so on.

In this chapter, we will move up in terms of API abstraction and look at the chart-related API, which we can use for visual presentation. In this chapter, you will learn the following topics:

- Creating cartesian charts — line, bar, area charts
- Creating polar charts — pie chart
- Creating spacefilling charts — gauge chart
- Theming your charts
- Engaging users with gestures

Types of charts

Sencha Charts supports the following types of charts:

- **Cartesian charts**: These charts are based on a two-dimensional coordinate system or the cartesian coordinate system. This is where the position of a point is determined based on its (x, y) coordinate. Typical examples are area charts, bar charts, and line charts.

- **Polar charts**: These charts are based on the polar coordinate system. This is a two-dimensional coordinate system where the position of a point in the plane is determined based on its distance from a fixed point and angle from a fixed direction. Typical examples are Pie and Radar.

- **Spacefilling charts**: These charts fill the entire space/area of the chart. For example, Treemap and Gauge.

The following screenshot shows the different types of Sencha Charts:

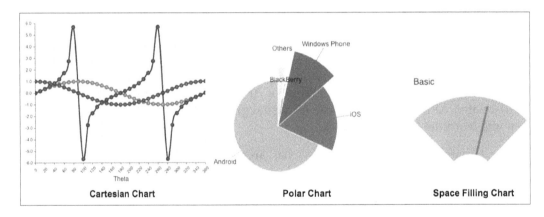

Anatomy of a chart

A chart has different areas. Each area has its own name. These names will act as the terminology that Sencha Charts will use and they will be used throughout this book. The following diagram depicts a cartesian chart created using Sencha Charts with its different areas:

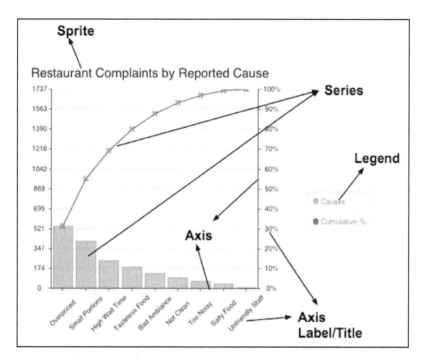

Let's take a look at a few of the terminologies highlighted in the preceding figure:

- **Sprite**: This is an object that is rendered on a drawing surface — Ext.draw. Surface — which we discussed in the previous chapter. Sencha Charts offers many different types of sprite, such as arc, circle, rectangle, path, and text, all of which are used internally to create different types of chart. They can also be added directly to a chart. In the preceding diagram, a text sprite is used to show the chart title.

- **Series**: This class is very specific to the type of chart that we want to draw. For example, Sencha Charts uses area series to draw area charts, whereas bar series draw bar charts. Based on the samples/data, the series determines what sprites need to be added to the surface. It also takes care of animations and provides events that can be used to increase user interactivity with a chart. For this reason, in Sencha Charts, there is no bar chart class. Rather, there is a bar series, which determines how many bars need to be drawn on the surface using a rectangle sprite.

- **Axis**: This is drawn based on the type of chart. For example, for a cartesian chart, *x* and *y* axes are drawn, whereas for a polar chart, angular and radial axes are drawn. Sencha Charts provides three types of axis:

  - `numeric`: This works with continuous numeric data. For example, sales amount.

  - `time`: This works with continuous date or time data. For example, hours, days, months, and years.

  - `category`: This works with a finite dataset and places these datasets evenly on the axis. For example, sales quarters.

- **Legend**: This gets the color and text from each of the series that is rendered in a chart. You can hide/show a particular series by toggling the legend icon for that series.

- **Chart**: Based on the type of chart, this draws legend and axes, and uses series to draw the sprites on its surface. Every chart has various surfaces of its own.

Now that we have our terminology set, let's see how we can create some real charts using Sencha Charts.

Creating a cartesian chart

We will start by making a cartesian chart. A cartesian chart must have axes and a series along with the dataset:

1. Create a project using Sencha Cmd with `SCE` as the application name.

2. Edit the `app/view/main/Main.js` file and replace its contents with the following code to create a cartesian chart that shows quarterly sales and quarterly orders:

```
Ext.define('SCE.view.main.Main', {
    extend: 'Ext.container.Container',

        xtype: 'app-main',

    layout: {
        type: 'fit'
    },

    items: [{
        xtype: 'cartesian',
        title: 'Chart',
        height: 500,
        width: 500,
```

```
    insetPadding: 40,
    legend: true,
    store: {
        fields: ['month', 'sales', 'order'],
        data: [
            { month: 'Q1', sales: 100, order: 20 },
            { month: 'Q2', sales: 250, order: 120 },
            { month: 'Q3', sales: 75, order: 40},
            { month: 'Q4', sales: 120, order: 25}
        ]
    },
    axes: [{
        title: 'Sale',
        type: 'numeric',
        position: 'left',
        fields: ['sales']
    },
    {
        title: 'Order',
        type: 'numeric',
        position: 'right',
        fields: ['order'],
        maximum: 200
    },
    {
        title: 'Quarter',
        type: 'category',
        position: 'bottom',
        fields: ['month']
    }],
    sprites: [{
        type: 'text',
        text: 'Quaterly Sales and Orders',
        font: '22px Helvetica',
        width: 100,
        height: 20,
        x: 40,
        y: 20
    }],
    series: [{
        type: 'bar',
        xField: 'month',
        yField: 'sales',
        title: 'Sale'
    }, {
        type: 'area',
        xField: 'month',
```

```
            yField: 'order',
            title: 'Order',
            showMarkers: true,
            marker: {
                type: 'circle',
                radius: 5
            },
            style: {
                opacity: 0.5
            }
        }]
    }]
});
```

In the preceding code, we added a `cartesian` chart component to the container as its child. This component prepares a surface internally, onto which, the sprites are drawn.

To feed the data to the chart, we configured a `store` with the `data` samples.

To show the legend on the chart, all we have to do is set the `legend` config to `true` on the chart component. The rest of the logic is to show that the legend is internal to the chart.

We configured three axes on the chart; two `numeric` and one `category` type. The `numeric` axes display the numbers; for example, sale figures and order figures. The `category` axis shows the quarters.

For each of the axes, we set their `position` values and associate them to a `data` field on the `store`.

The `series` configuration on a chart component is used to configure the different series that we want to show. In this case, we have added two series; the `bar` series to show the quarterly sales and the `area` series to show quarterly orders. The following configuration on the area series shows circular markers:

```
showMarkers: true,
marker: {
    type: 'circle',
    radius: 5
},
```

Finally, the only thing left is to show the report title on the top of the chart. For this, we configured the `text` sprite on the chart component and positioned it at the top.

3. Deploy and access the application in a browser. You will see the following output with three axes, a legend, two series, and a title, as shown in the following figure:

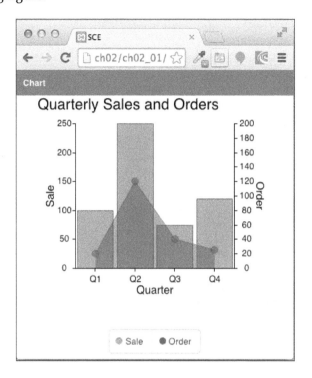

Creating a polar chart

Pie and Radar are out-of-the-box polar charts provided by Sencha Charts. These charts use the polar coordinate system to draw sprites. Pie series does not require an axes configuration. However, Radar series does require `axes` configuration, one `radial` and another `angular`.

Let's see how we create a polar chart with a `pie` series.

Create a project using Sencha Cmd with `SCE` as the application name. Edit the `app/view/main/Main.js` file and replace its contents with the following code:

```
Ext.define('SCE.view.main.Main', {
    extend: 'Ext.container.Container',

        xtype: 'app-main',

    layout: {
```

```
              type: 'fit'
        },

        items: [{
            xtype: 'polar',
            title: 'Chart',
            height: 500,
            width: 500,
            store: {
                fields: ['sample', 'value'],
                data: [
                    { sample: '1', value: 100 },
                    { sample: '2', value: 250 },
                    { sample: '3', value: 175}
                ]
            },
            series: [{
                type: 'pie',
                xField: 'value',
                label: {
                    field: 'sample',
                    renderer: function(txt) {
                        return "Sample " + txt;
                    }
                }
            }]
        }]
    });
```

In the preceding code, we added a `polar` type of chart component to the container. This `polar` chart component contains the logic necessary to render data using the polar coordinate system logic.

The `axes` configuration is not needed in this case, as the pie series does not have anything to render on either the radial or angular axes.

We have used the `pie` series to draw the chart. It splits the pie based on the sample value. It distributes proportionately 360 degrees among each sample pie based on its value. The `renderer` method on the label allows us to customize the label text.

The following screenshot shows the pie chart produced by the preceding code:

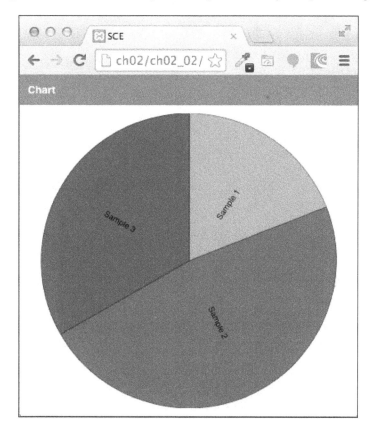

Creating a spacefilling chart

A spacefilling chart does not have a coordinate requirement. It occupies the available area with the chart. Treemap, heatmap, and gauge charts are some examples. Treemap and heatmap charts do not come with Sencha Charts. Gauges, however, does come along with it. Let's see how to use it in an application.

Create a project using Sencha Cmd with SCE as the application name. Edit the app/view/main/Main.js file and replace its contents with the following code:

```
Ext.define('SCE.view.main.Main', {
    extend: 'Ext.container.Container',

        xtype: 'app-main',

    layout: {
```

```
            type: 'fit'
        },

        items: {
            xtype: 'spacefilling',
            series: {
                type: 'gauge',
                minimum: 100,
                maximum: 800,
                value: 400,
                donut: 30,
                needle: true,
                colors: ['orange', 'blue']

            }
        }
    });
```

The preceding code uses a `spacefilling` chart component to show a gauge with a needle.

The following output is produced when you access the application in a browser:

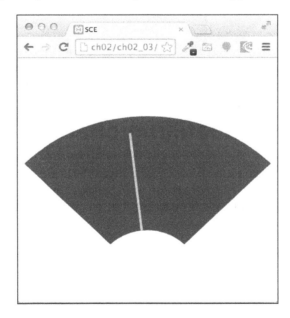

Theming your chart

By default, Sencha Charts uses a theme to draw series, axis, labels, and legends. This is the reason we did not have to provide any color or style related configuration to the charts that we created in the earlier topics.

This default theme may not be suitable for your application because the colors do not gel well with your application theme. There are three ways in which we can theme our chart:

- **Using various style-related configurations**: Sencha Charts provides various configurations at different levels to style different sections of a chart. For example, the chart component has configurations such as `background`, `cls`, `gradients`, and `style`. Similarly, axis has `background`, `grid`, `style`, and `renderer`. Series has `background`, `animation`, `colors`, `markerSubStyle`, `style`, `subStyle`, `useDarkerStrokeColor` and `renderer`. Likewise, label has `display`, `color`, `font`, `orientation`, and `renderer` configurations to style it.

- **Creating a custom theme and applying it to the chart**: In this approach, rather than configuring different style-related attributes on different sections of the chart, we define them in a single place, as a custom theme, and apply them to the chart using its theme configuration.

- **Creating a new chart theme using SASS**: In this approach, we create a theme by overriding the theme's SASS variables and style-related code. This is discussed in *Chapter 7, Theming*.

In this section, we will see how to define a custom theme and apply it to the charts.

1. To define a new custom chart, we will have to extend the `Ext.chart.theme.Base` class, as follows:

```
Ext.define('SCE.view.chart.theme.Awesome', {
    extend: 'Ext.chart.theme.Base',
    singleton: true,
    alias: 'chart.theme.awesome',

    series: {
     defaults: {
       style: {
         lineWidth: 2
       }
     },
     bar: {
       animation: {
         easing: 'bounceOut',
         duration: 1000
```

```
        },
        style: {
            fillStyle: '#6F5092',
            strokeStyle: '#6F5092'
        }
      },
      area: {
            style: {
                fillStyle: '#64BD4F',
                strokeStyle: '#00904B'
            }
      }
    },
    axis: {
      defaults: {
        style: {strokeStyle: 'red'}
      },
      left: {
        title: {fillStyle: '#6F5092'},
        label: {fillStyle: '#6F5092'}
      },
      right: {
        title: {fillStyle: '#00904B'},
        label: {fillStyle: '#00904B'}
      }
    }
});
```

2. Save the preceding code in the app/view/chart/theme/Awesome.js file.

   In the preceding code, we have configured the styles for the bar and area series where we have set the color to be used to fill and stroke them. For the bar series, we have additionally configured the animation config to animate it. The defaults config applies to all the series in a chart to which this theme is applied.

   The entire axes-related configuration is set using the axis config where we defined the common style using defaults and axis-specific styles using their positions, left and right. The alias name is a shortcut name to refer to the class and it is this alias, awesome, which is used on the chart.

   Once the theme is defined, we will go back to the SCE.view.main.Main class and make some changes.

3. Add the theme class to its requires array so that the class is loaded, as follows:

   ```
   requires: ['SCE.view.chart.theme.Awesome'],
   ```

4. Set the `theme` configuration used on the chart component, as highlighted in the following code snippet:

```
xtype: 'cartesian',
title: 'Chart',
theme: 'awesome',
height: 500,
...
...
```

5. Run the application and you will see the following output based on the new custom theme that we have applied to the chart:

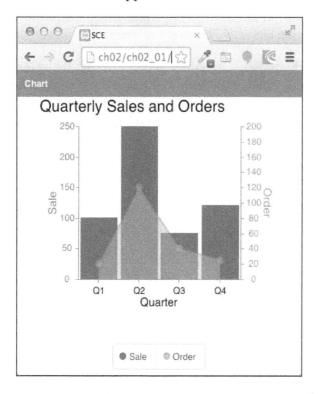

Note that the legend picked up the series color automatically.

Similarly, you can style other series such as pie, radar, 3D pie, and chart background. You can also change the default color set that the chart uses to draw the series for different samples, by configuring the `colors` config which we used in our spacefilling chart example.

Engaging users with gestures

Now, we are able to create some great looking charts and style them with our `Awesome` theme. However, it would be great if we could enable our users to interact with the chart, so they can get more information out of the presentation. For example, to figure out the sales amount for Q2, the user would have to look at the *x* axis and *y* axis labels to get the Q2 sales figure. However, if we can intercept the `mouseover` event on the bar and show the information in a tooltip, getting the same information is quicker.

Sencha Charts provides `interactions` to build interactivity in your chart. This is implemented by the base abstract class, `Ext.chart.interactions.Abstract`.

There are various built-in interactions implemented by the framework that we can leverage, such as `Crosshair`, `CrossZoom`, `ItemHighlight`, `ItemInfo`, `PanZoom`, `Rotate`, and `RotatePie3D`. While `Crosshair`, `CrossZoom`, and `PanZoom` interactions apply to cartesian charts, `Rotate` applies to polar charts, `ItemHighlight` and `ItemInfo` apply to all types of charts, and `RotatePie3D` is specific to 3D pie.

 If your requirement is beyond this list, say you want to allow the user to freely draw anything on the chart, then you can implement your own custom interaction, which we will discuss in *Chapter 8, Working with Touch Gestures*.

Let's see how we can use some of these interactions in our cartesian chart. Every interaction has an alias name and we add it to the `interactions` config on a chart, as shown in the following code in bold:

```
xtype: 'cartesian',
title: 'Chart',
theme: 'awesome',
interactions: ['crosshair', 'itemhighlight'],
height: 500,
    . . .
    . . .
```

The `itemhighlight` interaction expects us to specify the `highlight` configuration for the desired series. So, on the `bar` series, add the following code to style the series when it has to be highlighted and the tooltip that will be displayed on mouse over:

```
. . .
title: 'Sale',
highlight: {
   strokeStyle: '#094144',
   fillStyle: '#60D5DB'
},
```

```
tooltip: {
    trackMouse: true,
    style: 'background: #fff',
    renderer: function(storeItem, item) {
        this.setHtml(storeItem.get('month') + ': INR ' + storeItem.
get('sales'));
    }
}
```

On running the application, when the mouse hovers over a bar, you will see that the bar is highlighted based on the color that we specified. Also, the tooltip appears, showing the quarter and the corresponding sales amount. Additionally, when you hold the left mouse button and drag it, you will see the crosshair lines. On a touch screen, tapholding and dragging will show the crosshair. The following screenshot shows the output, one showing the tooltip, and the other showing the crosshair lines:

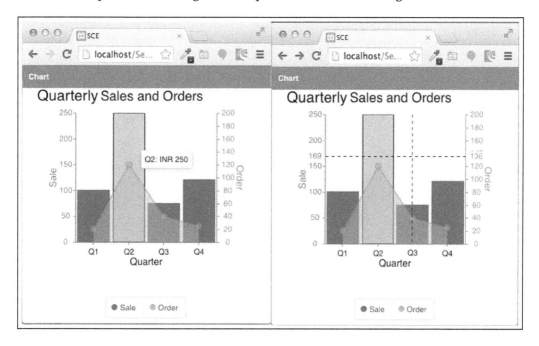

Similarly, you can configure other interactions to make your chart more engaging and effectively present the information to your user.

Summary

In this chapter, we discussed the subclasses of the `Ext.chart.AbstractChart` API— `CartesianChart`, `PolarChart`, and `SpaceFillingChart`—which provide much better abstraction for charting as compared to the low-level `Ext.draw.Surface` API that we saw in the previous chapter. We looked at the three concrete implementations of the `AbstractChart` API—`CartesianChart`, `PolarChart`, and `SpaceFillingChart`—and discussed their specific behavior and how we can use them in our application to create different charts. In the latter half of the chapter, we looked at the different ways to style or theme a chart and you learned how to define a custom theme and use the same on a chart. Finally, we made our chart interactive using `interactions` and `tooltip`.

In the next chapter, we will delve deeper into the Sencha Charts package and learn its architecture.

3
Sencha Charts Architecture

Ext JS 5.0 has introduced a new and powerful Sencha Charts package for data visualization. Though the old Ext JS Charts is still supported, it will be replaced eventually by Sencha Charts. Sencha Charts has evolved from Sencha Touch and due to this, it has built-in support for touch events which can be used by a user to interact with charts, in ways such as tap, pinch, and so on. Sencha Charts renders charts as SVG or HTML5 Canvas, where appropriate (for example, VML in IE8). However, we will limit our discussion to Canvas and SVG.

Charts are a great way to provide a quick overview of different KPIs, which makes it an essential part of any enterprise solution. While Sencha Charts comes with various built-in charts that can get us started with data visualization, to create a perfect decision-making solution for your customer, you will need to look beyond them. Also, when you have to do that, it is critically important to understand the extensible capabilities that the Sencha Charts package offers in terms of customizing and extending an existing chart, and finally, creating a new custom chart.

In this chapter, we will dive deeper into the Sencha Charts architecture and understand the ingredients and process for creating a custom chart.

In this chapter, we will discuss:

- Different types of charts offered by the Sencha Charts package
- Control flows to construct and render charts
- An example to implement the Sencha Charts architecture.

Architecture of Sencha Charts

Sencha Charts supports the following type of charts:

- **Cartesian chart**: This works with the cartesian coordinate system where we work with the x and y axes

- **Polar chart**: This works with the polar coordinate system where we work with angular axis (circle) and radial axis (towards radius)

- **Spacefilling chart**: This creates a chart that fills the complete area of the charts

The following screenshot shows examples of each type of chart that Sencha Charts offers:

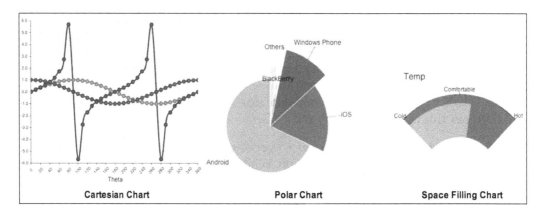

| Cartesian Chart | Polar Chart | Space Filling Chart |

The Sencha Charts package implements the different types of chart using the following major classes:

- **Chart** (`Ext.chart.AbstractChart`): This is a common class that implements the different types of charts, as described previously. Based on the type of chart, the class generates the axis. For example, for a cartesian chart, it generates the x and y axes, whereas for a pie chart, it will generate the pie using the polar coordinate system, and so on. The chart class manages the following common features across different types of charts and series:
    - Axis
    - Legend
    - Theme
    - Grid
    - Interaction
    - Events

- **Series** (Ext.chart.series.Series): Sencha Charts defines bars, columns, lines, areas, and so on as a series. A series contains the logic for how the data will be rendered on a chart. This draws a set of sprites to generate the desired visual output. For example, the line series draws a path that draws a line graph. This also fires events, which are relayed by a chart. It also supports showing tooltips on mouseover.

- **Sprite** (Ext.draw.sprite.Sprite): This is a class to draw different shapes, such as a rectangles, ellipses, paths, text, images, and so on. It offers the basic building block to render series. Bigger sprites can be created by combining basic shapes. For example, a line series uses a line sprite, which combines a path, circle, and so on. Additionally, a sprite has support for a gradient and modifier such as an item highlighter.

- **Draw** (Ext.draw.Container): This is the main container in which the chart is rendered. It extends the Ext.panel.Panel class. On this draw container, the surface is rendered. It also provides the API to download a chart as an image of a PDF document.

- **Surface** (Ext.draw.Surface): A chart is divided into various layers of surfaces, which are described later. Each layer takes care of rendering specific information. A surface class uses the underlying engine to render the chart as HTML5 Canvas or SVG. The engine is detected based on the browser's capability to support canvas or svg.

- **Engine** (Ext.draw.engine.Canvas/Ext.draw.engine.Svg): This is the lowest level class in the Sencha Charts stack. It encapsulates the differences between the HTML5 Canvas and SVG APIs and provides a common API to the surface class.

The following diagram shows how these classes are stacked together:

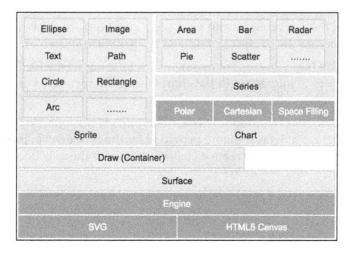

In the preceding diagram, we depicted the most common and high-level classes that are used to create charts in a Sencha application. The Surface API is not just stacked beneath the `draw` container. It is also available to directly add drawing elements to it. This is the reason we have the Surface API directly accessible to the Chart layer.

Besides the major classes that we have discussed previously, there are a few additional useful classes that are worth knowing, for when we intend to create custom charts. These classes are as follows:

- **Axis** (`Ext.chart.axis.Axis`): This class is responsible for rendering the chart axis based on the type of data that will be rendered on the axes. There are three types of axis classes, `Numeric`, `Category`, and `Time`, offered by Sencha Charts. As the name suggests, `Numeric` is used to render the data that is numeric in nature; these are usually factual; for example, sales in a monthly sales chart. The `Category` axis is used to render the category data, for example, a month in a monthly sales chart. The `Time` axis is a numeric axis but it works on a date field. The axis uses two classes, `Segmenter` and `Layout`, to segment the axis based on the data values and calculates the major ticks, minor ticks, minimum, maximum accordingly. It then uses the layout to position them on the axis.

- **Legend** (`Ext.chart.Legend`): This class shows the chart legends at the specified position. It extends the data view component. Generally, there may not be a need to customize it as the value is automatically derived from `store` that was passed to the series. However, there may be a situation where you have to customize it. For example, when you want to show the product's logo and name in the legend on a product-wise sales chart.

- **Markers** (`Ext.chart.Markers`): The axis uses this class to draw the tick markers.

- **Grid** (`Ext.chart.grid.*`): The axis uses this class to draw grid lines. For example, the `horizontal` and `vertical` grid lines are shown on a cartesian chart, whereas the `circular` and `radial` grids are shown on a polar chart.

- **Interaction** (`Ext.chart.interactions.Abstract`): Sencha Charts allows users to interact with the charts using interactions. For example, `pan` and `zoom`.

- **Theme** (`Ext.chart.theme.Theme`): This class is responsible for theming a chart. There is a default theme provided by the framework, but this class can be used or extended to create a custom theme for the axis line, label, series, and so on.

The following diagram shows how the preceding classes are connected to each other and the interactions between them:

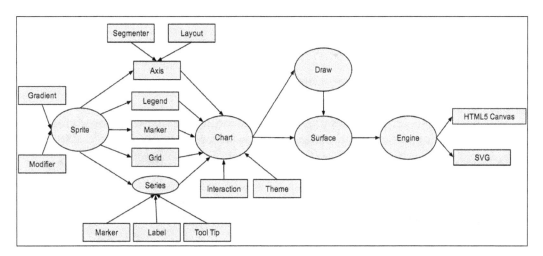

The classes are common for Sencha Ext JS as well as Sencha Touch. However, the platform-specific differences (for example, Interaction) are encapsulated inside their specific class by extending a common base class.

One last thing in the architecture is the different layers in Surface. In *Chapter 1, Fundamentals of Sencha Charts*, we used the main layer to render the chart and used the overlay layer to render the crosshair lines. Sencha Charts creates similar layers to render different content on each layer.

A chart is divided into various layers of surfaces and each surface is used to render a special type of content. The layering is controlled using z-indices. The following diagram shows the different layers, their z-index orders, and what gets rendered:

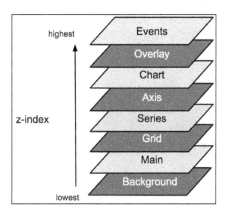

The following list describes what is rendered on each of the surfaces:

- **Background**: This renders the chart background. We can either fill it with a color or add a sprite to it.

- **Main**: This contains the chart and shows the GPL watermark for a GPL version of the SDK.

- **Grid**: This renders the grid lines, vertical and horizontal, for a cartesian chart, whereas angular and radial for polar charts.

- **Series**: This renders the series' sprites including the markers. For example, the bars of a bar series are drawn on this surface.

- **Axis**: This renders the different types of axes, which are `numeric`, `category`, and `time`.

- **Chart**: This renders the title text and sprites passed as a `sprites` config to a chart. It also takes care of showing the text based on the RTL (right-to-left) value.

- **Overlay**: This renders on top of the series surface and is used to show crosshair lines and the tooltip. It is part of the series.

- **Events**: This is, currently, unused.

Now that we have looked at the overall architecture of Sencha Charts, classes, and how they work together, let's review some of the chart implementations to see the architecture in action.

A walkthrough of an existing CandleStick chart

Let's look at the Stock App that comes along with Sencha Touch SDK and see how these classes have been used to achieve the desired behavior. When you download and extract the Sencha Touch SDK, you will find the source code in the `examples/stockapp` folder.

The following diagram depicts the Stock App output where we have highlighted the chart-related items:

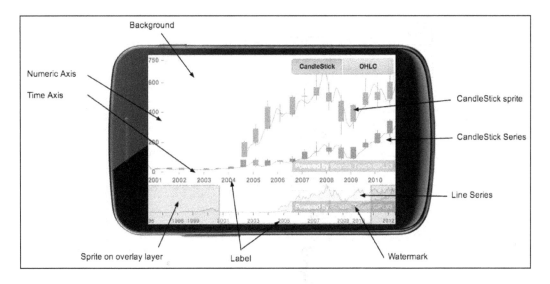

Design of the Stock App

The Stock App has two charts for the following purposes:

- To show the CandleStick/OHLC chart
- To show the preview with a range mask to allow the user to resize the preview area

There is a certain event handling mechanism put in place to sync the CandleStick chart with the preview area that is visible to the user by dragging the handlers on the RangeMask. We will limit our focus on how the CandleStick chart and the RangeMask custom sprites are implemented.

The following diagram shows the classes that are involved in the application and how they are connected:

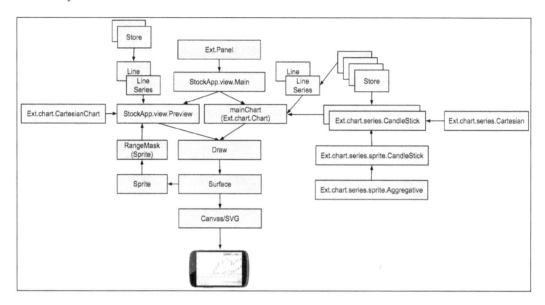

In the preceding diagram, we highlighted the classes that are responsible for showing the candlestick chart on the top, and the preview area at the bottom which shows two line series and a custom sprite—RangeMask—added to the `overlay` surface of the `preview` chart.

The `CandleStick` series does not do much. It borrows the capabilities from the cartesian series and adds four additional configs—`openField`, `closeField`, `highField`, and `lowField`—which are used to draw the CandleStick/OHLC sprites. Based on these field values, the data will be extracted from the passed store to render the series. This series uses the `CandleStick` sprite class to take care of the actual drawing.

The CandleStick sprite's `renderAggregates` method takes care of rendering the sprites based on the CandleStick/OHLC graph logic. It uses the `ohlcType` config, which defaults to `candlestick`, to decide whether it has to draw the sprites as per the CandleStick or the OHLC graph. The method calculates the open, high, low, and close values with respect to the screen coordinates, and calls private method `candlestick` or `ohlc` based on the `ohlcType` value. These private methods use the `moveTo` and `lineTo` APIs of the underlying Canvas/SVG engine to draw the graph.

The `RangeMask` render method extends `Ext.draw.sprite.Sprite`, which is the base class for drawing any sprite, such as a circle, path, and so on. The `RangeMask` render method implements the logic to draw the rectangular areas along with handlers, which can then be dragged by a user to change the preview area. This sprite is added to the overlay layer so that it appears on top of the series as the z-index of the overlay surface is higher than that of the series surface.

The sequence diagram

Let's look at the sequence of calls that are made across the main classes that we listed earlier to achieve the desired output.

Let's break it into two parts:

- Construction and initialization
- Rendering

Construction and Initialization

In the construction and initialization stage, the different classes are instantiated and initialized and they are prepared to enter into the rendering stage.

Preview with RangeMask

The following diagram shows the sequence of steps carried out to initialize a Preview area with RangeMask:

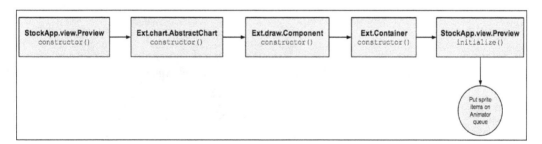

The `Preview` constructor constructs a cartesian chart with the configured `axes`, `series`, and `sprites`. The `RangeMask` is added as a sprite to the chart's `overlay` surface.

After the construction, the `initialize` method is called, which is the lifecycle method of a component. The framework calls this method during the initialization of a component. The `initialize` method initializes the chart, first, by calling the superclass `initialize` method. After this, it registers the touch event handlers on the chart element to handle the movement of the `RangeMask` handler and also sets the FX-related property on the `RangeMask`.

During this phase, the sprite items are added to the Animator queue, which will run and render them on the screen.

CandleStick

The following diagram shows the initialization steps for CandleStick chart:

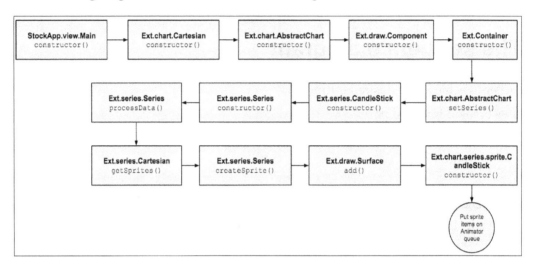

The Main class constructs a cartesian chart with the CandleStick series. The sprites for the CandleStick series are constructed using Ext.chart.series.sprite. CandleStick and are placed on the Animator queue.

Rendering

In the rendering stage, the actual visual output produced, is visible on the screen, as shown in the section, *A walkthrough of an existing CandleStick chart*:

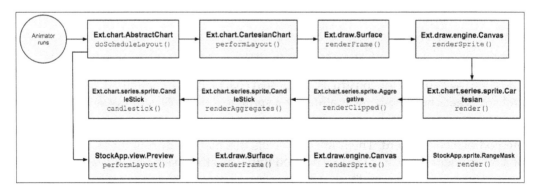

The sprites related to the `Preview` chart and the `CandleStick` charts were kept on the queue. The queue is scheduled to run when any change is detected on a chart, such as chart construction, when series or axes information is updated, or resizing is detected. One path shows the rendering sequence for the `Preview` chart, whereas the other one shows the sequence for the `Main` chart (primarily, the `CandleStick` chart).

A walkthrough of a polar chart – radar

The radar series is rendered using the polar chart as it works with the polar coordinate system. It uses the radial and angular axes to determine the position of a point. The following diagram depicts Radar where we have marked different areas, such as the axis, legend, series, and sprite:

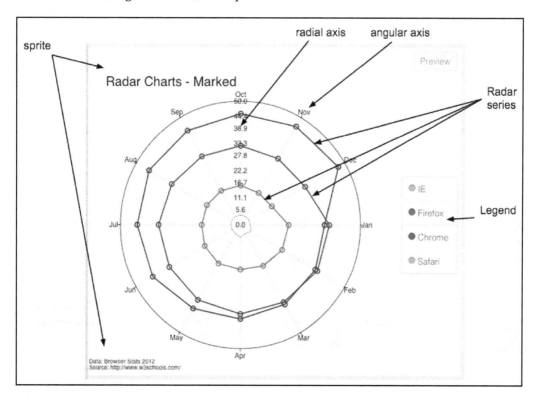

In the preceding diagram, the Radar series is used with two axes:

- The `numeric` axis along the radius to show the browser usage data
- The `category` axis along the angular direction to show the month

The following diagram shows the different classes involved in the construction and initialization of a chart with the Radar series and the control flow:

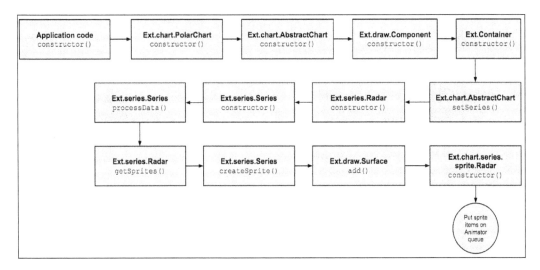

This is similar to the CandleStick series that we saw earlier, except that in place of CartesianChart, PolarChart is used and in place of the CandleStick series (and related sprites), the Radar series' (and related sprites) classes are used.

When it comes to rendering a polar chart, again, the steps are consistent with that of a cartesian chart, and hence the following diagram will be very similar to the rendering of the CandleStick series. The only difference is that CandleStick has additional sprite-related logic that it builds on top of the Aggregative sprite class, whereas Ext.chart.series.sprite.Radar offers the complete sprite-related logic for the Radar series. The following diagram depicts the rendering process of a polar chart with the Radar series:

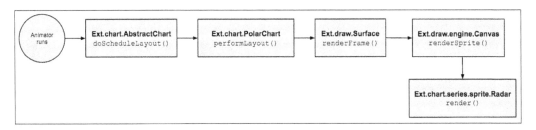

A walkthrough of a spacefilling chart – gauge

A spacefilling chart does not have an axis, and fills the chart area with the drawing. The following diagram shows a gauge series rendered inside a spacefilling chart:

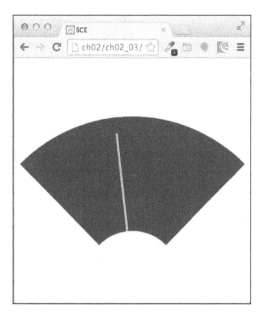

A spacefilling chart does not do much. It relies on the series to provide the final set of sprites and renders them on the surface.

The following diagram depicts the construction and initialization process of a spacefilling chart with the Gauge series:

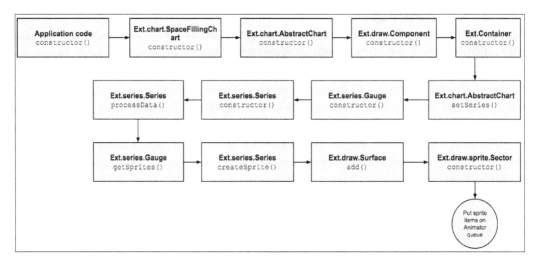

The following diagram shows the rendering process for a spacefilling chart:

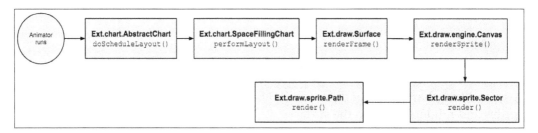

Summary

This chapter was dedicated to Sencha Charts architecture where we saw the different classes that are part of the architecture, their responsibilities, and how they are connected to provide the required functionality. We validated the architecture by reviewing the implementation of all the three types of charts: cartesian, polar, and spacefilling.

With this architectural and design background, we will start creating different types of custom charts in the next chapters.

4

Creating a Custom Cartesian Chart

With the launch of Ext JS 5, Sencha introduced a new and more powerful Sencha Charts package, which has built-in support for touch events. This means you can use touch gestures to interact with the charts. Sencha Charts has been built with performance in mind and will render charts as SVG or HTML5 Canvas, where appropriate (or VML in IE8). You can refer to the Ext JS 5 Charts Kitchen Sink to test drive and learn more about Sencha Charts.

In this chapter, you will learn how to create custom cartesian charts using the new Sencha Charts packages:

- Create a custom sprite
- Create a custom series
- Create a custom chart
- Use the newly created custom chart in an application
- Demonstrate how to create a new financial chart with the **MACD (Moving Average Convergence/Divergence Oscillator)** indicator.

Creating a new financial chart

In this section, you will see how to create a custom stock chart—MACD—that is a momentum oscillator offering trend following and momentum. It fluctuates above and below the zero level.

 You can read more about this at http://en.wikipedia.org/wiki/MACD.

What is this chart all about?

Let's derive the technical requirements for the MACD chart, which we will use as a foundation to implement our custom chart.

For the MACD chart, based on the stock data that contains open, high, low, and close values for different time instances, the following values need to be calculated:

- 12-day **Exponential Moving Average (EMA)**
- 26-day EMA

Once the preceding values are calculated, the MACD-related values will be calculated for a record, by applying the following formulae:

- *MACD line = 12-day EMA - 26-day EMA*
- *Signal line = 9-day EMA of MACD line*
- *MACD histogram = MACD - Signal line*

After the MACD line, signal line, and histogram values have been calculated, we need to draw a chart between them and the time, as shown in the following sample MACD chart:

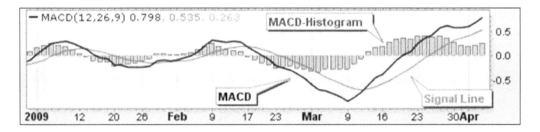

Credit: StockCharts.com

MACD contains two line series; to draw the MACD and the signal lines, and one bar series to draw the histogram.

Technically, to create a MACD chart, we would consider the following requirements as the scope for this chapter:

- It takes the following parameters:
    - `period1`: This is typically set to 12 days. However, it needs to be configurable.
    - `period2`: This is typically set to 26 days. However, it needs to be configurable.

- ° signalPeriod: This is typically set to 9 days. However, it needs to be configurable.

- ° closeField: This is the data field that contains the stock closing value. It is defaulted to close. However, it needs to be configurable.

- The numeric axis indicates the 0 (zero) level mark

- A dotted horizontal line is drawn at the 0 level mark

- A MACD line is created as a line series

- A MACD signal line is created as a line series

- Line series are created with different colors to be able to differentiate one from another

- A histogram is created that oscillates around the 0 level horizontal line

- The chart will be created based on Sencha Charts package architecture.

For brevity, we have excluded axis, legend, marker, tooltip, and theme customization, which are discussed in *Chapter 7*, *Theming*.

Structuring the MACD chart design

The following diagram shows the specific classes that we need to implement to create a MACD chart and discusses how they are connected with Sencha Charts classes:

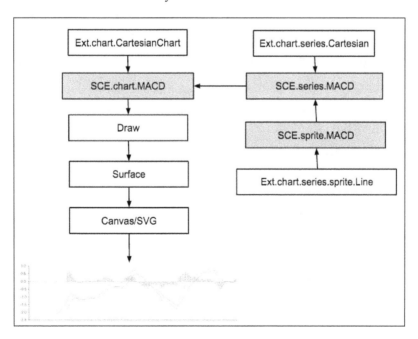

The classes highlighted with a grey background are related to MACD, which we will implement soon. The classes are as follows:

- `SCE.chart.MACD`: This extends the `CartesianChart` class and provides MACD chart-specific extensions by accepting the parameters described earlier, and uses them in the chart logic.

- `SCE.series.MACD`: This class will contain the logic needed to use the MACD-specific parameters and the `store` to calculate the sample values that draw the MACD line, signal line, and the histogram. It sets them in the store so that the respective line and bar series can use them.

- `SCE.sprite.MACD`: This class takes care of drawing the zero level line, which it does by extending the `Line` sprite class.

You will learn more about these classes when we implement them.

Implementing a MACD chart

With the high-level requirements and design in place, let's start with the implementation. First, we will look at the low-level sprite class, which renders the drawing for a series.

SCE.sprite.MACD

This class implements the MACD sprite logic to draw the 0 level line. This 0 level line is used to show how the values oscillate around the level.

In this class, we have two important methods:

- `drawYLine`: This draws a horizontal line at a specified y level

- `renderAggregates`: This is the main method that calculates the zero level and draws the line at y=0 by calling the `drawYLine` method

Here is the complete implementation of the class:

```
Ext.define('SCE.sprite.MACD', {
    alias: 'sprite.macd',
    extend: 'Ext.chart.series.sprite.Line',

    /**
     * @private Override {@link Ext.chart.series.sprite.
Line#renderAggregates}
     */
    renderAggregates: function (aggregates, start, end, surface, ctx,
clip, rect) {
```

```
        this.callParent(arguments);

        var me = this,
            attr = me.attr,
            matrix = attr.matrix,
            yy = matrix.getYY(),
            dy = matrix.getDY();

        var pixelAdjust = attr.lineWidth * surface.devicePixelRatio /
2;

        pixelAdjust -= Math.floor(pixelAdjust);

        var zeroLevel = Math.round(0 * yy + dy) - pixelAdjust;

        me.drawYLine(ctx, rect[2], zeroLevel, true);
    },

    /**
     * @private
     * Draws a line parallel to X-axis
     * @param ctx SVG or Canvas context
     * @param x length of the line
     * @param y ordinate where the line needs to be drawn
     * @return
     *
     */
    drawYLine: function(ctx, x, y, dashed) {
        ctx.beginPath();
        ctx.moveTo(0, y);
        ctx.lineTo(x, y);
        ctx.closePath();

        var linedash;
        if (dashed) {
            linedash = ctx.getLineDash();
            ctx.setLineDash([3]);
        }
        ctx.stroke();

        //reset the dash style
        if (dashed) {
            ctx.setLineDash(linedash);
        }
    }
});
```

In the preceding code, the `drawYLine` method uses the `moveTo` and `lineTo` methods of the `ctx` object, to draw the line. These methods are translated to SVG or the Canvas API by Sencha Charts based on the underlying browser/device capability.

The preceding class extends the `Ext.chart.series.sprite.Line` class as we will use its capability to draw a line. We have overridden the `renderAggregates` method to first draw the line, by calling the parent `renderAggregates` method using the `this.callParent` call. After the line is drawn, we draw the horizontal line at zero level using the `drawYLine` method. The zero level `y` value is calculated after transforming the user coordinate system to the device coordinate system using the following line, which relies on the transformation matrix and is described as follows:

```
var zeroLevel = Math.round(0 * yy + dy) - pixelAdjust;
```

 You can read more about the transformation matrix at http://en.wikipedia.org/wiki/Transformation_matrix.

The following diagram depicts how a user perceives a coordinate system, in contrast to how the device coordinates system is actually laid out:

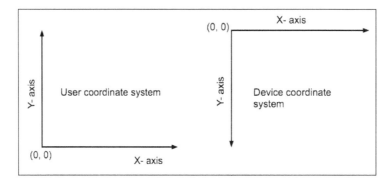

Now, with the sprite class in place, let's move on to our next class—`SCE.series.MACD`—where we will implement the series-related logic.

SCE.series.MACD

This series class accepts the `store` and the following specific parameters:

- The value of `period1` should be defaulted to `12`
- The value of `period2` should be defaulted to `26`
- The value of `signalPeriod` should be defaulted to `9`
- The value of `closeField` should be defaulted to `close`

The `store` contains the `close` field that this series class uses to calculate the line, signal line, and histogram values of MACD based on different periods—`period1`, `period2`, and `signalPeriod`.

The MACD line is calculated using the following formula:

MACD Line = (12-day EMA - 26-day EMA)

EMA is calculated from the `closeField` values.

Once the EMAs are calculated based on `period1` and `period2`, the signal line value is calculated using the following formula:

Signal Line = 9-day EMA of MACD Line

Finally, we create the histogram value based on the values that we calculate for the MACD line and signal line, using the following formula:

MACD Histogram = MACD - Signal Line

The series code is as follows:

```
Ext.define('SCE.series.MACD', {
    extend: 'Ext.chart.series.Cartesian',
    alias: 'series.macd',
    seriesType: 'macd',  //sprite type for this series

    config: {
        /*
         * Data field containing the close value. Defaults to "close"
         */
        closeField: "close",
        /*
         * First period to calculate EMA of close price. Defaults to 12
         */
        period1: 12,
        /*
         * Second period to calculate EMA of close price. Defaults to
26
         */
        period2: 26,
        /*
         * Period to calculate EMA for MACD Signal. Defaults to 9
         */
        signalPeriod: 9
    },

    /*
```

```
 * Creates a MACD series
 * @param {Object} [config] Configuration
 */

constructor: function (config) {

    var me = this;

    var store = Ext.getStore(config.store);

    var records = store.getRange();

    var closes = Ext.Array.pluck(Ext.Array.pluck(records, "data"),
config.closeField);

    var p1 = config.period1, ema1Arr = [], ema1 = 0, prevEma1;
    var p2 = config.period2, ema2Arr = [], ema2 = 0, prevEma2;
    var sp = config.signalPeriod, ema3 = 0, prevEma3;
    var close, macd, macdArr = [];

    //calculate multipliers
    var mult1 = 2/(p1 + 1);
    var mult2 = 2/(p2 + 1);
    var mult3 = 2/(sp + 1);

    store.each(function (item, index, length) {
        close = item.data[config.closeField];

        //Calculate MACD
        if (index >= p1) {
            if (index == p1) {
                ema1 = Ext.Array.mean(Ext.Array.slice(closes, 0,
index));
            } else {
                ema1 = (close - prevEma1) * mult1 + prevEma1;
            }

            prevEma1 = ema1;
        }

        if (index >= p2) {
            if (index == p2) {
                ema2 = Ext.Array.mean(Ext.Array.slice(closes, 0,
index));
```

```
        } else {
            ema2 = (close - prevEma2) * mult2 + prevEma2;
        }

        prevEma2 = ema2;
    }

    //MACD Line: (12-day EMA - 26-day EMA)
    if (ema1 && ema2) { //this is not clear whether we shall
consider the records where p1 < p2. TODO: verify from other resources
        macd = ema1 - ema2;

        item.data.macd = macd;

        macdArr.push(macd);
    }

    //Calculate MACD Signal line
    //Signal Line: 9-day EMA of MACD Line
    var l = macdArr.length;
    var maxP = Ext.Array.max([p1, p2]);
    var p = maxP + sp;
    if (index >= p) {
        if (index == p) {
            ema3 = Ext.Array.mean(Ext.Array.slice(macdArr, 0,
sp));
        } else {
            ema3 = (macd - prevEma3) * mult3 + prevEma3;
        }

        prevEma3 = ema3;

        item.data.sigmacd = ema3;

        //calculate diff for MACD histogram
        //MACD less MACD signal line
        item.data.histmacd = macd - ema3;
    }

});

this.callParent(arguments);
    }
});
```

In the preceding code, we implemented the constructor for the series, to calculate the `macd` value to draw the MACD line, `sigmacd` to draw the MACD signal line, and `histmacd` to draw the MACD histogram. Once these values are set in the `store` records, they are ready to be used by the different series' logic to draw them on the screen.

 Ideally, we do not touch the store that has been passed to the code. Rather, we will have our own internal store and use it in the logic.

Now, we are left with one last class — `SCE.chart.MACD` — the chart that lets us create a MACD chart in an application.

SCE.chart.MACD

The chart class extends the `CartesianChart`, where it expects a `numeric` type axis to be specified by the caller. It uses the specified numeric axis to draw the MACD values. This class sets the following MACD-related additional `axis` configs in its `initConfig` method, which is called at the time of the class initialization:

- `fields`: This is the field that will be rendered on the `numeric` axis; it is set to `macd`, `sigmacd`, and `histmacd`. Based on these fields, the value range for the *y* axis is calculated.

- `series`: This adds a `line` series to draw the signal line based on the `sigmacd` value on the record, and a `bar` series to draw the histogram based on the `histmacd` value set on the record by the `SCE.series.MACD` class.

Here is the complete MACD chart class implementation:

```
Ext.define("SCE.chart.MACD", {
    extend: 'Ext.chart.CartesianChart',
    requires: ['SCE.series.MACD',
               'SCE.sprite.MACD'],

    xtype: 'macdchart',

    initConfig: function(config) {

        Ext.Array.each(config.axes, function(axis, index, recs) {
            if (axis.type === 'numeric') {
                Ext.apply(axis, {

                    fields: ['macd', 'sigmacd', 'histmacd']

                });
```

```
            }
        });

        //add a line series for MACD Signal line and a bar for MACD
    Histogram
        config.series.push({
            store: config.series[0].store,
            type: 'line',
            xField: 'date',
            yField: 'sigmacd',
            style: {
                stroke: 'rgba(255,102,102,0.75)',
                miterLimit: 1
            }
        }, {
            store: config.series[0].store,
            type: 'bar',
            xField: 'date',
            yField: 'histmacd',
            style: {
                stroke: 'rgba(228,124,124,0.75)',
                fillStyle: 'rgba(228,124,124,0.75)'
            }
        });

        this.callParent(arguments);
    }
});
```

We are almost done, except for one final step where we will use the preceding chart in an application and see it in action.

Using MACD in an application

In the previous section, we defined a MACD chart with the `'macdchart'` xtype. Let's see how we can use it in our sample application.

To use the preceding chart in an application, we can either instantiate it using the `Ext.create` call, or use the `xtype` or `xclass` config. For example, here is the code showing the configuration for adding this chart to an Ext JS container as one of its items:

```
{
    xclass: 'SCE.chart.MACD',
    height: 250,
    background: 'white',
```

```
    series: [
        {
            store: Ext.create('SCE.store.Apple', {}), //'Apple',
            type: 'macd',
            xField: 'date',
            yField: 'macd',
            closeField: "close",
            period1: 12,
            period2: 26,
            signalPeriod: 9,
            style: {
                stroke: 'rgba(67,174,175,0.75)',
                miterLimit: 1
            }
        }

    ],
    axes: [
        {
            type: 'numeric',
            position: 'left'
        },
        {
            type: 'category',
            position: 'bottom',
            fields: ['date'],
            style: {
                strokeStyle: '#666',
                estStepSize: 150
            },
            dateFormat: 'Y',
            segmenter: {
                type: 'time',
                step: {
                    unit: 'y',
                    step: 1
                }
            },
            label: {
                fontSize: 10,
                fillStyle: '#666'
            }
        }
    ]
}
```

The following graph shows a CandleStick chart with a MACD indicator:

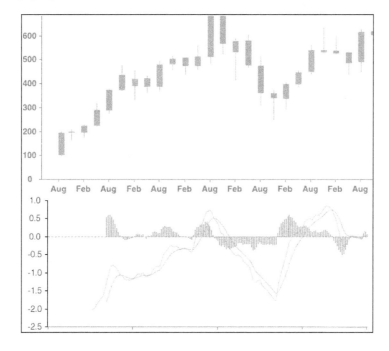

Summary

In this article, we discussed how to create a custom stock chart based on the cartesian coordinate system. We implemented a custom chart, series, and a sprite for a MACD indicator that is commonly used by Stock analysts. The implementation demonstrated Sencha Charts' important classes, their responsibilities, interactions, and how you can create a custom chart. Subsequently, you learned how to use the newly created cartesian custom stock chart in an Ext JS 5 application.

Next, we will see how to create a custom polar chart and use it in our application.

5
Creating a Custom Polar Chart

In the previous chapter, we saw how to create a custom cartesian chart using Sencha Charts. In this chapter, we will look at how a polar chart works and how to create a custom polar chart. We will create a custom polar chart — Market Clock — where we will use the polar coordinate system to create a 12-hour clock showing the opening and closing times of different stock exchanges.

In this chapter, you will learn how to create custom polar charts by:

- Creating a custom sprite
- Creating a custom series
- Creating a custom polar chart
- Taking care of legends, centering, and resizing
- Using the custom polar chart in an application

Creating a Market Clock

In this section, you will see how to create a Market Clock, shown here, where we show the duration for which a stock exchange is open. It's a great visual tool to keep track of the opening and closing times of different stock exchanges.

The clock given at `http://market24hclock.com/` is a great example of a stock market clock as it quickly gives an idea about the opening and closing times of different exchanges.

The following diagram shows the Market Clock that we will create in this chapter:

What is this chart all about?

The stock market chart that we will build in this chapter has the following requirements:

- It should show a 12-hour clock
- For each stock exchange, it should show a sector on top of the clock
- Each sector should represent the duration for which an exchange is open
- The Exchange name should be shown on the sector
- Each sector should use a unique color

Based on the preceding requirements, let's start with the design and then we will move on to the implementation.

Structuring the design

The following diagram shows the specific classes that we need to implement to create the Market Clock, and how they are connected with the Sencha Charts classes:

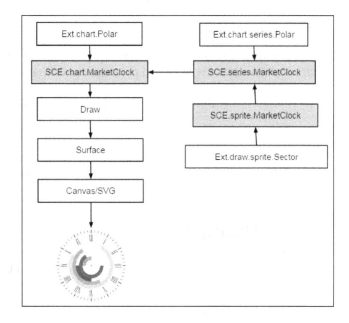

The classes highlighted with a gray background are related to the Market Clock chart, which we will implement in a while. The following list describes the chart-specific classes:

- SCE.chart.MarketClock: This class extends the polar chart class and it will handle the display of the 12-hour clock, on top of which, the series' sprites will be rendered.

- SCE.series.MarketClock: This class will have the logic that is used for the market timings data, which is stored inside the chart store—SCE.store. MarketTimings—to create the Market Clock. It uses the SCE.sprite. MarketClock sprite class to create a sprite for each market.

- SCE.sprite.MarketClock: This class takes care of drawing a market's operation timings, which it does by extending the Sector sprite class. It also shows the market name on the respective sectors.

You will learn more about these classes during their implementation.

Implementing the Market Clock

With the design in place and the classes and their responsibilities identified, let's get down to their implementation. We will implement the following classes:

- Store: `SCE.store.MarketTimings`
- Sprite: `SCE.sprite.MarketClock`
- Series: `SCE.series.MarketClock`
- Chart: `SCE.chart.MarketClock`

After the preceding classes are implemented, we will update the `Main` class to add our custom polar chart and use the new series to produce the Market Clock.

To start with, we need to generate a project by running the following Sencha Cmd command:

```
sencha generate app SCE<application path>
```

Now, let's go to the `app` folder of the newly generated project code and start creating and updating the specific classes.

SCE.store.MarketTimings

The `SCE.store.MarketTimings` class is the store class, which is used on the `SCE.chart.MarketClock` polar chart instance. The store uses inline data. Here is the record structure:

- `market`: This specifies the market name.
- `opening`: This specifies the opening time of a market. The value is assumed to be in h:iA format, for example, 09:30AM.
- `closing`: This specifies the closing time of a market. The value is assumed to be in h:iA format, for example, 09:30AM.

Here is the definition of the store class:

```
Ext.define('SCE.store.MarketTimings', {
  extend: 'Ext.data.Store',
  alias: 'store.markettimings',
  config: {
    storeId: 'MarketTimings',
    fields: ['market', 'opening', 'closing'],
    data: [
      { market: 'India', opening: '09:00AM', closing: '12:00PM'},
      { market: 'Sydney', opening: '03:00AM', closing: '11:00AM'},
```

```
        { market: 'Singapore', opening: '06:00AM', closing: '09:00AM'},
        { market: 'USA', opening: '05:00AM', closing: '11:00AM'},
        { market: 'Malaysia', opening: '01:00AM', closing: '10:00AM'}
    ]
  }
});
```

The preceding store definition uses an inline model, as the fields have been defined here. You can define a separate model and use it on the store.

SCE.sprite.MarketClock

The `SCE.sprite.MarketClock` class is responsible for creating a sprite for each market, shown as follows:

For each sprite, it creates the following:

- A sector with a color
- A market name text along the sector arc path

Here is the implementation of the sprite class:

```
Ext.define('SCE.sprite.MarketClock', {
  alias: 'sprite.marketclock',
  extend: 'Ext.draw.sprite.Sector',

  render: function (surface, ctx, clip, rect) {
    var me = this,
    attr = me.attr,
    itemCfg = {},
    changes;

    var startAngle = Math.min(attr.startAngle, attr.endAngle);
    var endAngle = Math.max(attr.startAngle, attr.endAngle);
    var startRho = Math.min(attr.startRho, attr.endRho);
    var endRho = Math.max(attr.startRho, attr.endRho);
```

```
        if (attr.renderer) {
          itemCfg = {
            type: 'sector',
            centerX: attr.centerX,
            centerY: attr.centerY,
            margin: attr.margin,
            startAngle: startAngle,
            endAngle: endAngle,
            startRho: startRho,
            endRho: endRho
          };
          changes = attr.renderer.call(me, me, itemCfg, me.rendererData,
            me.rendererIndex);
          me.setAttributes(changes);
          me.useAttributes(ctx, clip);
        }

        // Draw the sector
        me.callParent([surface, ctx, clip, rect]);

        this.drawTextAlongArc(ctx, attr.text, attr.centerX, attr.centerY,
startRho
          + 10, startAngle, endAngle - startAngle);
      },

    drawTextAlongArc: function(ctx, text,x,y,radius,startAngle,
sectorSize){
      var radianPerLetter = Math.PI/30;
      ctx.save();
      ctx.translate(x,y);
      ctx.rotate(startAngle + ((sectorSize - (radianPerLetter*text.
length))/2));

      for(vari=0;i<text.length;i++){
        ctx.save();
        ctx.translate(radius, 0);

        ctx.translate(10, -10);

        ctx.rotate(1.4)
        ctx.translate(-10, 10);
        ctx.fillStyle = 'black';

        ctx.fillText(text[i],0,0);
        ctx.restore();
        ctx.rotate(radianPerLetter);
      }
```

```
        ctx.restore();
    }
});
```

The MarketClock sprite class extends the sector sprite and overrides the render method. The render method does the following functions:

- Calls the parent class method — render — to create the sector
- Calls the drawTextAlongArc method to add market name text to the sector

To create a sector, the sprite relies on the following sector attributes, which are sent by the MarketClock series:

- centerX: This is the center coordinate of the sprite on the *x* axis.
- centerY: This is the center coordinate of the sprite on the *y* axis
- startAngle: This is the starting angle of the sector for a market
- endAngle: This is the ending angle of the sector for a market
- startRho: This is the starting point of the radius of the sector arc
- endRho: This is the ending point of the radius of the sector arc

The following diagram depicts the terms used in the preceding list:

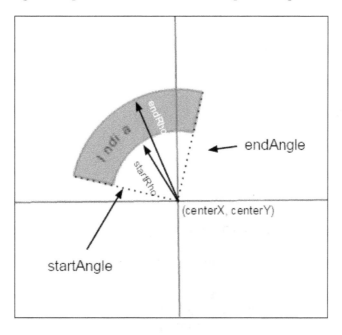

The `drawTextAlongArc` method adds a market name along with the sector arc. This method is a bit more involved, as it uses the Canvas APIs to render the text along with the arc. Unlike SVG, Canvas does not have direct support to draw text along a path. This method uses the axis translation and rotation to calculate the position of each letter in the market name and draws it using the `fillText` API of the Canvas class. You can see some issues with the calculation as some names, for example, India, do not render properly. I will leave it as an exercise for you to redefine the logic needed to render the text along the path.

Now, let's look into the `MarketClock` series, which uses this sprite class.

SCE.series.MarketClock

The `SCE.series.MarketClock` class creates the Market Clock where it uses the `MarketClock` sprite to create each of the stock exchange's timings.

Here is the implementation of the class:

```
Ext.define('SCE.series.MarketClock', {

    extend: 'Ext.chart.series.Polar',

    requires: ['SCE.sprite.MarketClock'],

    type: 'marketclock',
    alias: 'series.marketclock',
    seriesType: 'marketclock',

    getSprites: function () {
      var me = this,
      store = me.getStore();
      if (!store) {
        return [];
      }


      var items = store.getData().items,
      length = items.length,
      sprites = me.sprites, sprite, i;

      var openingDt, closingDt;
      var anglePerHr = (Math.PI*2)/12;
      var anglePerMin = (Math.PI*2)/60;

      for (i = 0; i< length; i++) {
```

```
          sprite = sprites[i];
          if (!sprite) {
            sprite = me.createSprite();

              //calculate sector startAngle and endAngle based
              //on the opening and closing timings
            openingDt =  Ext.Date.parse(items[i].get('opening'), 'h:iA');
            closingDt =  Ext.Date.parse(items[i].get('closing'), 'h:iA');

            var openingHr = Ext.Date.format(openingDt, 'G') * 1;
            var openingMin = Ext.Date.format(openingDt, 'i') * 1;
            var closingHr = Ext.Date.format(closingDt, 'G') * 1;
            var closingMin = Ext.Date.format(closingDt, 'i') * 1;

            var startAngle = anglePerHr*openingHr + anglePerMin*openingMin

              (Math.PI/2);
            var endAngle = anglePerHr*closingHr + anglePerMin*closingMin -
              (Math.PI/2);

            var attr = {
              text: items[i].get('market'),
              startAngle: startAngle,
              endAngle: endAngle,
              startRho: 30*i + 50,
              endRho: 30*i + 80
            };

            sprite.setAttributes(attr, true);
          }
        }

      return me.sprites;
    },

  getDefaultSpriteConfig: function() {
    return {
      type: this.seriesType,
      centerX: 340,
      centerY: 340
    };
  }
});
```

The preceding class uses the `MarketClock` sprite by associating it, using the `seriesType` property on the series. The `getDefaultSpriteConfig` method returns the base sprite configuration, which is used by the framework to create a sprite when the following method is called as part of the `getSprites` method:

```
me.createSprite();
```

We have defaulted to the `centerX` and `centerY` attributes for the clock as a part of its default sprite configuration. However, you can parameterize them so that they can be passed by the caller at the time of instantiating the series. Refer to *Chapter 4, Creating a Custom Cartesian Chart*, to see how to parameterize these values.

The `getSprites` method is called during the series lifecycle to get the list of sprites corresponding to the series. The method does some of the following checks, initially, to ensure that the store is valid:

```
if (!store) {
  return [];
}
```

The method loops through the store items, which contain the markets and their timings data, and creates sprites for them. It calculates the following values and sets them as sprite attributes so that the `MarketClock` sprite's `render` logic can use them:

- `text`
- `startAngle`
- `endAngle`
- `startRho`
- `endRho`

Again, we are directly using the model field names to extract the market and their timings. However, you can parameterize them, as discussed earlier.

SCE.chart.MarketClock

The `SCE.chart.MarketClock` class extends the `PolarChart` and shows the clock image as the chart background so that the series' sprites can be rendered on top of it.

The following is the implementation of the chart class:

```
Ext.define('SCE.chart.MarketClock', {

  extend: 'Ext.chart.PolarChart',
  xtype: 'marketclock',

  constructor: function(config) {

    config.background = {
      type: 'image',
      src: 'resources/images/Clock.jpg'
    };

    this.callParent(arguments);
  }

});
```

The preceding class implements the constructor to set the background configuration on the `PolarChart`, so that it can be rendered by the parent class.

SCE.view.main.Main

The `SCE.view.main.Main` class was generated by Sencha Cmd when the project was generated. Edit it and replace the code with the following code:

```
Ext.define('SCE.view.main.Main', {
  extend: 'Ext.container.Container',

  requires: [
    'SCE.chart.MarketClock',
    'SCE.series.MarketClock',
    'SCE.store.MarketTimings'
  ],

  xtype: 'app-main',

  items: [{
    xtype: 'marketclock',
    height: 700,
    width: 700,
    store: Ext.create('SCE.store.MarketTimings'),
    series: [{
      type: 'marketclock',
```

```
            angleField: 'data'
        }]
    }]
});
```

The preceding code uses the `marketclock` chart and adds `marketclock` as a series to it. The chart uses the `SCE.store.MarketTimings` store to feed the exchange data to the series.

This completes our implementation of the Market Clock polar chart. Deploy the application and access it in your browser. We will see the Market Clock as the output.

Adding legend support

Now that the clock is ready, let's add some bells and whistles to it. Imagine that your clock shows the timings for numerous markets and you would like to see the legend for them, so that you can hide/view certain markets by clicking on the legend. For example, the following figure depicts how we have hidden the Singapore market timing by deselecting it on the legend:

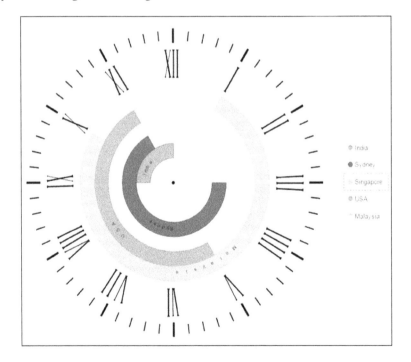

The base `AbstractChart` class supports:

- Creating the legend
- Rendering it on the screen based on the specified position, and controlling the series visibility based on the legend item selection or deselection

Displaying the legend

To both, enable and see the default legend on a chart, all we have to do is set the following configuration on our `marketclock` chart instance:

```
xtype: 'marketclock',
legend: {
docked: 'right'
},
height: 700,
...
```

The preceding `legend` configuration tells the chart to show the legend on the right-hand side of chart.

Now, when we run the application, our default legend does not look that great and is not even close to what we would like to see. Besides, when you deselect the legend item, it will hide all the market timing slots, as shown here:

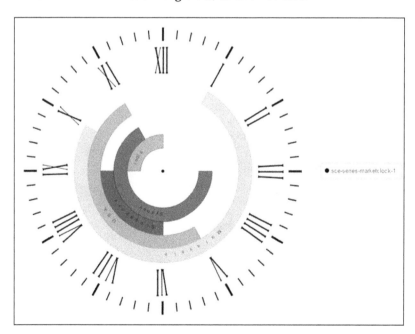

This is primarily because our custom series has not provided the legend information as expected by the Sencha Charts framework. Let's review how a legend is constructed and rendered in Sencha Charts.

The `AbstractChart` base class calls the `provideLegendInfo` method on a series to get the legend-related data and passes it to the `Ext.chart.Legend` class, which draws and positions the legend on the screen. The `Legend` class subclasses `LegendBase`, which is a DataView, in Ext JS. It uses an `XTemplate` to create the legend items. The `XTemplate` uses the following data fields:

- `name`: This is used to display the label for a legend item. In our case, we will show the exchange name.

- `mark`: This controls the background of a legend item. In our case, we will use the same color that we used to draw the time sector for a market; for example, for India, it will be green.

- `disabled`: This disables a legend item if its series is hidden. We will not be using it, so, we will default it to `false` so that all the legend items are enabled and the user can click on them to select or deselect.

So, let's provide our own version of the `provideLegendInfo` method. Here is the implementation of the method which will be a member method of the `SCE.series.MarketClock` class:

```
provideLegendInfo: function (target) {
  var me = this,
  store = me.getStore();
  if (store) {
    var items = store.getData().items,
    i, style;

    for (i = 0; i<items.length; i++) {
      style = me.getStyleByIndex(i);
      target.push({
        name: items[i].get('market'),
        mark: style.fillStyle || 'black',
        disabled: false
      });
    }
  }
}
```

The `AbstractChart` class the preceding method by passing an empty array to it as an argument. We have used the formal parameter – `target` – for it. The method iterates the chart's `store` records and prepares the legend data for them. Legend data contains the `name`, `mark`, and `disabled` fields. The `name` field is set to the market name using the `market` field on the record. The `mark` field is set to the sector color. Once the legend data is created, it is added to the target array so that it is available to the `AbstractChart` logic, where it adds this data to its `legendStore`.

Refresh the application and you will see the neat legend displayed on the right-hand side of our market clock.

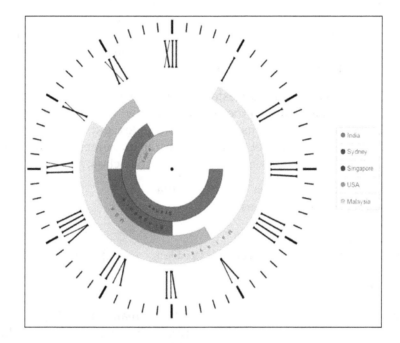

Great! Now try selecting a legend item. The legend item changes its color to show that it is deselected but the corresponding market sector does not disappear. It is because we have some more work to do.

Controlling the sprite visibility

Now, let's see how we can link a legend item selection/deselection to its market sector visibility. Before we jump into the implementation, let's first understand how the control flows inside Sencha Charts.

We know that the `LegendBase` class uses a DataView to render the legend. The `Legend` class, which is a subclass of `LegendBase`, handles the data view event when a legend item is selected. This handler updates the `disabled` field value on the `legendStore`. The `AbstractChart` class watches for any updates happening on `legendStore`. As soon as the `disabled` field value is updated, `AbstractChart` comes into action and its `onUpdateLegendStore` method is invoked. This method checks whether the selected legend record has the `series` field. If true, it calls `setHiddenByIndex` of the series and passes the `index` value of the selected legend item also stating whether it is disabled or enabled.

The `SCE.series.MarketClock` class extends the `Polar` series, which does not provide its own implementation of the `setHiddenByIndex` method. So, we will have to implement our own method of using the passed index and disabled/enabled flag to control the visibility of a market sector. Here is the implementation of the method, which we need to add to the `SCE.series.MarketClock` class:

```
setHiddenByIndex: function (index, value) {
  var sprites = this.sprites;

  if (sprites) {
    sprites[index].setAttributes({hidden: value}, true);
  }
}
```

The preceding method gets the sprites that we have created as part of its `getSprites` method call during the construction of the series. It then uses the `index` value to find the sprite corresponding to the selected legend item and sets the `hidden` attribute on it based on the second parameter named `value`.

Now when you run the application, you can see that our legend item selection/deselection has been linked with the show/hide of a market sector.

Centering the sectors

Try changing the height and width of the `SCE.view.main.Main` class from `700` to `750` on the `marketclock` chart and you will notice that the sectors are not centered anymore, as shown here:

To fix this issue, we will have to implement the `updateCenter` method on the `SCE.series.MarketClock` series class. This method is called by the `Ext.chart.PolarChartperformLayout` method at the time of rendering the series. It sets `center` and `radius` on the series. This set operation on the `center` config, calls the post hook method – `updateCenter` – of the `MarketClock` series. Here is the implementation of the method which we will add to the `MarketClock` series class:

```
updateCenter: function (center) {
  this.setStyle({
    centerX: center[0] + this.getOffsetX(),
    centerY: center[1] + this.getOffsetY()
  });
  this.doUpdateStyles();
}
```

In the preceding method, we updated the `centerX` and `centerY` attributes of the `MarketClock` sprite, which internally set it on the sector.

One more change we need to make is to the `getDefaultSpriteConfig` method on the `MarketClock` series class. We had hardcoded the `centerX` and `centerY` attributes to `340` pixels. We now change the values to `0`, highlighted as follows:

```
return {
  type: this.seriesType,
  centerX: 0,
  centerY: 0
};
```

Now, we can change the height and width of the `MarketClock` chart and the sectors will center properly.

Limiting the sector within the clock

Another issue is that the sector width is still fixed and will cause the sectors to render outside the clock's inner area if the chart's dimension goes below, say, `500` pixels, as shown here:

In the previous section, we discussed how radius is set on the series by the `PolarChart` class during the rendering. However, we did not use it to set the `startRho` and `endRho` attributes for each sector. To consider the radius and use it to calculate the new values for `startRho` and `endRho`, we will have to implement the `updateRadius` post hook method. Here is its method implementation:

```
updateRadius: function (radius) {
  var offsetFromCenter = 30;
  var sprites = this.sprites;
  var clockEdgeWidth = this.getChart().getWidth()*0.18;

  var sectorWidth = (radius - clockEdgeWidth -
    offsetFromCenter)/sprites.length;

  for (var i = 0; i<sprites.length; i++) {
    sprites[i].setAttributes({
      startRho: sectorWidth*i + offsetFromCenter,
      endRho:   sectorWidth*i + (offsetFromCenter + sectorWidth)
    }, true);
  }
}
```

The `clockEdgeWidth` value calculates the space that we need to leave, to be able to show the hour and minute tick lines. The `0.18` value has been calculated statistically. This takes into consideration the fact that if the chart is bigger, the clock image will be bigger and hence we will have to leave more space. However, if the chart is smaller, we will have to reduce the spacing.

The `sectorWidth` value represents the width of each sector.

The `for` loop iterates through each of the sprites—sectors—that were created, and sets their `startRho` and `endRho` attributes based on the runtime calculation.

Now that we have implemented the `updateRadius` method, let's clean up the `getSprites` method of the `MarketClock` series class by setting `startRho` and `endRho` to `0`, as highlighted in the following code snippet:

```
...
varattr = {
  text: items[i].get('market'),
  startAngle: startAngle,
  endAngle: endAngle,
  startRho: 0,
  endRho: 0
};
...
...
```

Change the chart height and width and you will notice that the sectors resize automatically. The following screenshot shows the output with different dimensions:

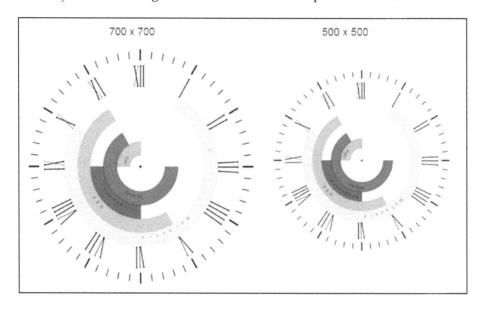

This completes our discussion on creating a custom polar chart.

Summary

In this chapter, we discussed how to create a custom polar chart where we saw how to extend the base `PolarChart` class to define our own polar chart. Also, we created a custom series to create a Market Clock using its own custom sprite class. The implementation demonstrated Sencha Charts' important classes, their responsibilities, interactions, and how you can create a custom polar chart. Also, we saw how to customize the legend and respond to its selection and deselection.

In the next chapter, we will see how to create the third type of chart, spacefilling.

6

Creating a Custom Spacefilling Chart

So far, we have seen how to create custom cartesian and polar charts. The third type of chart offered by Sencha Charts is **spacefilling**. A spacefilling chart offers a drawing area inside which anything can be drawn. It does not have coordinate systems like cartesian and polar charts. Examples of spacefilling charts are: Gauge, Treemap, Mindmap, and so on.

In this chapter, you will learn how to create custom spacefilling charts by:

- Creating a custom sprite
- Creating a custom series
- Using the custom series with a spacefilling chart
- Working with changing store data
- Scaling up/down different dimensions dynamically
- Deriving custom color coding logic

Creating a periodic table

In this section, you will see how to create a periodic table, shown as follows, where we show the atomic number and symbol for each element.

 You can read more about this at `http://en.wikipedia.org/wiki/Periodic_table`.

The following diagram shows the typical periodic table that we would like to create:

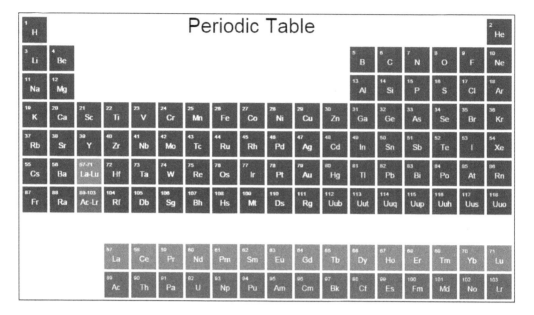

What is this chart all about?

From a charting perspective, our periodic table will have the following requirements:

- It has 18 columns
- For each element, we will show the atomic number and symbol
- Lanthanide and Actinide elements are displayed separately
- Lanthanides will be shown in green
- Actinides shall be shown in blue
- All other elements will be shown in black

With these requirements in place, let's get to the design and implementation of it.

Structuring the design

The following diagram shows the specific classes that we need to implement to create our periodic table and how they are connected with Sencha Charts classes:

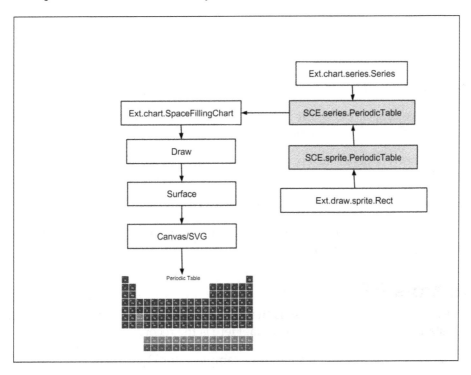

The classes highlighted with a gray background are related to the periodic table chart, which we will implement soon. The following list describes the chart-specific classes:

- SCE.series.PeriodicTable: This class will contain the logic necessary, to use the element data, which is stored inside the chart store, to create the periodic table. It uses the SCE.sprite.PeriodicTable sprite class to create a sprite for each element.

- SCE.sprite.PeriodicTable: This class takes care of drawing each element, which it does by extending the Rect sprite class. It shows the rectangle with text—showing the atomic number and symbol.

You will learn more about these classes during the implementation.

Implementing the periodic table

With the design in place and the classes and their responsibilities identified, let's get down to their implementation. We will implement the following classes:

- Store: `SCE.store.PTElements`
- Model: `SCE.model.PTElement`
- Sprite: `SCE.sprite.PeriodicTable`
- Series: `SCE.series.PeriodicTable`

After the preceding classes are implemented, we will update the `Main` class to add a spacefilling chart and use the new series to produce the desired outcome.

To start, we need to generate a project by running the following Sencha Cmd command:

```
sencha generate app SCE <application path>
```

Now, let's go to the `app` folder of the newly generated project code and start creating and updating the specific classes.

SCE.store.PTElements

The `SCE.store.PTElements` class is the store class, which is used on the spacefilling chart instance. The store uses inline data. Here is the record structure:

- `z`: This is the atomic number, for example, `1` for Hydrogen
- `mass`: This is the atomic mass
- `symbol`: This is the element symbol, for example, `H` for Hydrogen
- `name`: This is the full element name, for example, `Hydrogen`
- `group`: This is the group to which the element belongs, for example, `Helium` belongs to the Noble Gases group
- `row`: This is the row number of the element in the periodic table, for example, Lithium lies in row `2`
- `column`: This is the column number of the element in the periodic table, for example, Lithium lies in column `1`
- `items`: This is applicable to Lanthanide and Actinide series only

Here is the definition of the store class:

```
Ext.define('SCE.store.PTElements', {
   extend: 'Ext.data.Store',

   requires: ['SCE.model.PTElement'],

   model: 'SCE.model.PTElement',

   storeId: 'PTElements',
   data: [
   { z: '1', mass: null, symbol: 'H',name: 'Hydrogen', group: 'Other
Non-metals', row: 1, column: 1 },
   { z: '2', mass: null, symbol: 'He',name: 'Helium', group: 'Noble
Gases', row: 1, column: 18 },
   ....
   { z: '57-71', mass: null, symbol: 'La-Lu',name: 'Lanthanide', group:
'', row: 6, column: 3,
       items: [
          { z: '57', mass: null, symbol: 'La',name: 'Lanthanum', group:
'Lanthanides', row: 1, column: 1 },
          { z: '58', mass: null, symbol: 'Ce',name: 'Cerium', group:
'Lanthanides', row: 1, column: 2 },
   ....
       ]
   }]
});
```

SCE.model.PTElement

This SCE.model.PTElement class defines the model with fields, which will be used by the store class — SCE.store.PTElements. These fields are available on the data that is set on the store. In the implementation, we will use the following fields:

- z
- symbol
- name
- row
- column
- items

Here is the definition of the model class:

```
Ext.define('SCE.model.PTElement', {
   extend: 'Ext.data.Model',

   fields: ['z', 'mass', 'symbol', 'name', 'group', 'row', 'column',
```

```
'items']
});
```

SCE.sprite.PeriodicTableElement

The `SCE.sprite.PeriodicTableElement` class is responsible for creating a sprite of each element of the periodic table, as shown here:

For each sprite, this class fetches the data and performs the following:

* Creates a rectangle with a color
* Places the atomic number on the top-left corner
* Places the symbol name in the middle
* Places the element name at the bottom

Here is the implementation of the sprite class:

```
Ext.define('SCE.sprite.PeriodicTableElement', {
    alias: 'sprite.ptSeries',
    extend: 'Ext.draw.sprite.Rect',

    render: function (surface, ctx, clip, rect) {
        var me = this,
            attr = me.attr;

        // Draw the rectangle
        me.callParent([surface, ctx, clip, rect]);

        // Draw the labels
        me.placeLabels(surface, ctx, clip, rect, attr);

    },

    placeLabels: function(surface, ctx, clip, rect, attr) {
      surface.add({
        type: 'text',
        x: attr.x + 5,
        y: attr.y + 15,
        text: attr.z,
```

```
      fontSize: 10,
      fillStyle: 'white'
    });

    surface.add({
      type: 'text',
      x: attr.x + 25,
      y: attr.y + 35,
      text: attr.symbol,
      textAlign: 'center',
      fontSize: 15,
      fillStyle: 'white'
    });

      surface.add({
      type: 'text',
      x: attr.x + 25,
      y: attr.y + 45,
      text: attr.name,
      textAlign: 'center',
      fontSize: 9,
      fillStyle: 'white'
    });
    }
  });
```

The `PeriodicTableElement` sprite class extends the rectangle sprite class — `Ext.draw.sprite.Rect` and overrides the `render` method. The overridden `render` method does the following:

- Calls the parent class `render` method by calling `callParent()` to create the rectangle sprite
- Calls the private `placeLabels` method to add the atomic number, symbol, and name to the rectangle

We defined a private method, `placeLabels`. The `placeLabels` method adds the atomic number, name, and symbol as text sprites by adding them to the surface to which the rectangle was added.

Now, let's look into the `PeriodicTable` series, which uses this sprite class.

SCE.series.PeriodicTable

The SCE.series.PeriodicTable class creates the complete periodic table where it uses the PeriodicTableElement sprite to create each of the elements in a periodic table.

Here is the implementation of the SCE.series.PeriodicTable class:

```
Ext.define('SCE.series.PeriodicTable', {

   alias: 'series.periodictable',
   extend: 'Ext.chart.series.Series',

   requires: ['SCE.sprite.PeriodicTableElement'],

   type: 'periodictable',

   seriesType: 'ptSeries',

   getSprites: function() {
     var me = this,
            store = me.getStore(),
            i, j, ln, ln1,
            colors = ['#333', 'green', 'blue'];

        // The store must be initialized
        if (!store) {
            return [];
        }

        // Return cached sprites
        var chart = me.getChart(),
            animation = me.getAnimation() || chart && chart.
getAnimation(),
            sprites = me.sprites,
            spriteIndex = 0,
            sprite, attr, rendererData;

        if (sprites && sprites.length) {
            sprites[0].fx.setConfig(animation);
            return sprites;
        }

        // Create sprites
        var item = null, z = -1, subItems = [];
```

```
var items = store.getRange();

for (i = 0, ln = items.length; i < ln; i++) {
  item = items[i];

  var color = colors[0];

  z = item.get('z');

    //handle 57-71 and 89-103 differently
    if (item.get('items')) {
      subItems.push(item.get('items'));

      if (z === '57-71')
        color = colors[1];
      else
        color = colors[2];
    }

    attr = {
        fillStyle: color,
        strokeOpacity: 0,
        x: item.get('column') * 55,
        y: (item.get('row') - 1) * 55,
        z: z,
        mass: item.get('mass'),
        name: item.get('name'),
        symbol: item.get('symbol')
    };
    sprite = me.createSprite();
    sprite.setAttributes(attr, true);
}

for (i = 0, ln = subItems.length; i < ln; i++) {
  for (j = 0, ln1 = subItems[i].length; j < ln1; j++) {
    item = subItems[i][j];

    z = item['z'];
      attr = {
          fillStyle: colors[i+1],
          strokeOpacity: 0,
          x: (item['column'] + 3) * 55,
          y: (item['row']*(8 + i)) * 55,
          z: z,
```

```
                mass: item['mass'],
                name: item['name'],
                symbol: item['symbol']
            };
            sprite = me.createSprite();
            sprite.setAttributes(attr, true);
        }
    }

    return sprites;
},

getDefaultSpriteConfig: function() {
  return {
        type: this.seriesType,
        width: 50,
        height: 50
    };
  }

});
```

The SCE.series.PeriodicTable class uses the PeriodicTableElement sprite by associating it using the seriesType property on the series. The overridden getDefaultSpriteConfig method returns the base sprite configuration, which is used by the framework to create a sprite when the following method is called as a part of the overridden getSprites method:

```
me.callSprite();
```

The getSprites method is called during the series lifecycle to get the list of sprites corresponding to the series. The method does some checks, initially, to ensure that the store is valid:

```
if (!store) {
  return [];
}
```

The first for loop iterates through the store items and creates sprites for them. Also, it pushes items for an element, to a separate array — subItems — which contains the items for the Lanthanides and Actinides.

The second loop is as follows:

```
for (i = 0, ln = subItems.length; i < ln; i++) {
        for (j = 0, ln1 = subItems[i].length; j < ln1; j++) {
            item = subItems[i][j];
    . . .
    . . .
```

It iterates on the Lanthanide and Actinide items and creates sprites for them.

SCE.view.main.Main

This class was generated by Sencha Cmd when the project was generated. Edit it and replace the code with the following code:

```
Ext.define('SCE.view.main.Main', {
    extend: 'Ext.container.Container',

    xtype: 'app-main',

    requires: ['Ext.chart.SpaceFillingChart',
            'Ext.draw.Color',
            'SCE.store.PTElements',
            'SCE.series.PeriodicTable'],

    layout: {
        type: 'fit'
    },

    items: {
        xtype: 'spacefilling',
        colors: [],
        store: Ext.create('SCE.store.PTElements'),
        series: {
            type: 'periodictable'
        },
        sprites: {
            type: 'text',
            text: 'Periodic Table',
            fontSize: 40,
            x: 400,
            y: 40
        }
    }
});
```

The preceding code uses the `spacefilling` chart and adds `periodictable` as a series to it. The chart uses the `SCE.store.PTElements` store to feed the elements data to the series.

 We had to set the `colors` array to an empty array so that Sencha Charts does not pick up the colors for the sprites from its preset `colors` array.

This completes our implementation of the periodic table chart. Deploy the application and access it in your browser. We will see the periodic table as the output.

Though the output looks desirable, there are a few enhancements that are worth implementing to make our chart more configurable and usable. Let's look at the following aspects:

- How do we make the colors configurable at the group level?
- How do we respond to the store/data change?
- How do we respond to different chart dimensions?

Standardizing the color selection

The `getSprites` method of the series uses a predefined `colors` array with three color codes:

```
colors = ['#333', 'green', 'blue'];
```

However, behind the scenes, the series picks up the color based on the following:

- `style`
- `subStyle`
- theme `style`
- theme `subStyle`
- `colors`

While the `style` and `subStyle` values are read from the series configuration, theme `style` and `subStyle` are derived based on the chart theme configuration. If none of them are defined, it uses the `colors` array to determine the series color. More detailed discussion about these configurations will be discussed in *Chapter 7, Theming*.

Since we are not configuring `style`, `subStyle`, and `theme` on our chart, we will be using colors to render the sprites in the `PeriodicTable` series. However there is a problem, because all the sprites are created as part of a single series and hence all the elements in the periodic table will have the same color. But, what we require is to color code the elements based on their `group` names. This means, we need to modify the default approach for sprite color selection and derive it based on the element's `group` name.

The following are the steps to modify the default approach for sprite color selection:

1. Add a config — `groupColors` — to the `PeriodicTable` series, which contains a mapping of an element group name to its color code:

```
config: {
    groupColors: {
        'Other Non-metals': '#C3C3C3',
        'Alkali Metals': '#FE2E9A',
        'Alkali-Earth Metals': '#D1EF75',
        'Transition Metals': '#D7DF01',
        'Lanthanides': '#FFAE79',
        'Actinides': '#F89195',
        'Poor Metals': '#6CD3FE',
        'Semi Metals': '#CD8CCC',
        'Non-Metals': '#8584EA',
        'Noble Gases': '#FFC90D'
    }
},
```

2. Now, we will override the `getStyleByIndex` method of the `Ext.chart.series.Series` class to provide our custom logic to get the `fillStyle` based on the `group` name of a sprite identified using the `idx` parameter:

```
getStyleByIndex: function (idx) {
    var me = this,
        style = {fillStyle:  'black'};

    var sprite = me.sprites[idx];

    if (sprite) {
        style = {
            fillStyle: me.getGroupColors()[sprite.attr.group]
        }

        return style;
    }
}
```

This method uses the `group` attribute of a sprite to get the corresponding color from the `groupColors` map. It is called by the `doUpdateStyles` method of `Ext.chart.series.Series` class to get the style for a sprite.

3. Remove all the color-related logic from `getSprites` where we had defined a `colors` array and used it. Also, remove the `fillStyle` attribute that we were applying to the newly created sprite.

4. In step 2, the `getStyleByIndex` method requires the `group` attribute set on a sprite to be able to find its color. So, we will modify the `getSprites` method and pass the `group` attribute to the list of sprite attributes, as follows:

```
attr = {
    strokeOpacity: 0,


    name: item.get('name'),
    symbol: item.get('symbol'),
    group: item.get('group')
};


attr = {
    strokeOpacity: 0,


    name: item['name'],
    symbol: item['symbol'],
    group: item['group']
};
```

Save the changes and open the application in your browser. You will see the elements colored based on their group and the color that we associated to each group, as shown in the following screenshot:

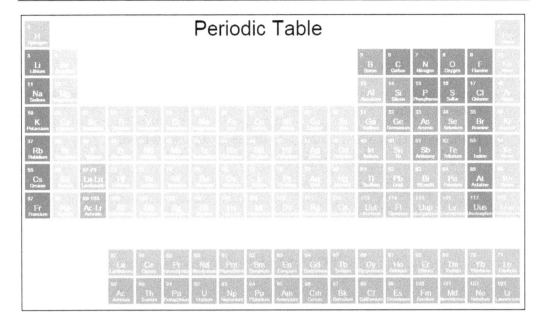

This looks much better and more colorful!

Working with store updates

Imagine that you plan to offer a multilingual periodic table where the element name will be presented, based on the user selected language. Effectively, in your application, based on the language selection, you would like to update the chart store with the language-specific element data and expect the chart/series to render the newly provided store/data. Let's see how we can get this working for a spacefilling chart.

1. First, let's define a new store for Hindi language where an element's name is in Hindi:

```
Ext.define('SCE.store.HindiPTElements', {
  extend: 'Ext.data.Store',

  requires: ['SCE.model.PTElement'],

  model: 'SCE.model.PTElement',

  storeId: 'HindiPTElements',
  data: [
  { z: '1', mass: null, symbol: 'H',name: 'हाइड्रोजन', group: 'Other
Non-metals', row: 1, column: 1 },
    { z: '2', mass: null, symbol: 'He',name: 'हिलियम', group: 'Noble
```

```
Gases', row: 1, column: 18 },

    ]
});
```

This store is very similar to the PTElements store, which contains the element name in English.

2. In the series class, we will now add the applyStore method:

```
applyStore: function(newStore, oldStore) {

    if (newStore) {
        var me = this;

        if (me.sprites) {
            Ext.destroy(me.sprites);
            me.sprites = [];
        }

        if (oldStore) {
            oldStore.setData(newStore.getData().items);
        }

        return oldStore;
    }
}
```

This method will be called when the setStore method is called on a periodictable series. The applyStore method does the following:

○ **Removes all the sprites**: This also removes the sprites from the Canvas

○ **Reinitializes the sprites property to an empty array**: This is needed, as getSprites is run again as soon as the store is updated with the new data, and setting it to an empty array will ensure that getSprites will regenerate all the sprites based on the updated store data

○ **Updates the data on the old store**: This will trigger the chart redraw and the sprites will be regenerated

○ **Returns the old store**: This has to be done as we have updated the oldStore data

3. Since a series class does not have a `store` config, the `applyStore` method will never be called. However, `store` is a config on the chart and hence we will define a new chart class and implement the `applyStore` method, as follows:

```
Ext.define('SCE.chart.PeriodicTable', {
    extend: 'Ext.chart.SpaceFillingChart',

    xtype: 'periodictable',

    applyStore: function(newStore) {

        if (newStore) {
            var me = this;

            var series = me.getSeries();
            if (series && series.length > 0) {
                series[0].setStore(newStore);
            }
            return newStore;
        }

    }
});
```

The preceding class extends the spacefilling chart and its `applyStore` method calls the `setStore` method on the `periodictable` series, which is the only series associated with this chart. The call to the `setStore` method will ensure that the series' `applyStore` method is called as part of the set operation.

> Since the series is modifying the store by changing its data, it might be a good idea to create a chart-specific store from the store passed to it by the caller. This can be done by cloning. This way, even if the store is shared across the chart and a grid, the grid will not get affected because of the data update.

The `applyStore` method of the chart class will be called when we call the `setStore` method on it. So, now all we have to do is implement the code to set the store based on language selection.

4. Modify the `Main` class to use the new `periodictable` chart as its child item rather than the `spacefilling` chart class:

```
items: [{
    xtype: 'periodictable',
```

```
            colors: [],
    ...
```

5. Now, the final step. Let's add a toolbar to the `Main` chart class with two buttons:

    ◦ **Hindi**
    ◦ **English**

    The handler for each of these buttons will set the language-specific store on the chart.

    We will add the toolbar as `dockedItems` to the `Main` class, as follows:

```
dockedItems: {
    xtype: 'toolbar',
    docked: 'top',
    items: [{
        xtype: 'label',
        text: 'Language:'
    },{
        text: 'Hindi',
        handler: function(btn) {
            var newStore = Ext.getStore('HindiPTElements');
            if (!newStore)
                newStore = Ext.create('SCE.store.
HindiPTElements');

            btn.up('app-main').down('periodictable').
setStore(newStore);
        }
    }, {
        text: 'English',
        handler: function(btn) {
            var newStore = Ext.getStore('PTElements');
            if (!newStore)
                newStore = Ext.create('SCE.store.PTElements');

            btn.up('app-main').down('periodictable').
setStore(newStore);
        }
    }]
},
```

The handler gets the language-specific store instance and sets it on the `periodictable` chart by calling the `setStore` method. This will call `applyStore` on the `PeriodicTable` chart, internally, which will set the new store on the `PeriodicTable` series. This triggers the `applyStore` call on the series class, which clears all the existing sprites and updates the existing store data with the new store data. Additionally, as soon as the store is updated, the `AbstractChart` class triggers the `redraw` method of the chart and we see the periodic table with element names displayed in the selected language.

The following screenshot shows the output produced when the user clicks on the **Hindi** button:

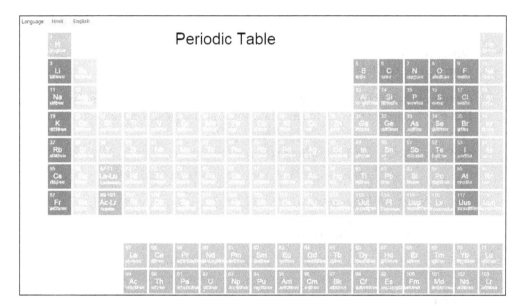

 Though the approach discussed here is in the context of a spacefilling chart, it can be applied to polar and cartesian charts, as well.

Resizing

The current implementation has the dimensions fixed for many things:

- Font size to render atomic number, name, and symbol
- Position of atomic number, name, and symbol texts with reference to the element's rectangle edges
- Size of the element's rectangle

This means our periodic table will not scale up/down based on the chart dimension. Try passing smaller or bigger values for the `height` and `width` configs for the `periodictable` chart in your `Main` class and observe the chart output. That's the exact problem we will solve in this section by making the following changes:

1. First, let's make the element size—`elSize`—and the gap between two adjacent elements—`gutter`—as configs on the `PeriodicTable` series class:

```
. . .
config: {
        elSize: 50,
        gutter: 5,
        groupColors: {
. . .
```

   Since, each element is represented as a square, we defined `elSize` rather than `width` and `height`.

2. Now, we make changes to the `getSprites` method of the series class to use these two configurations to calculate the x and y position for each element's sprite:

```
var rectWidth = me.getElSize() + me.getGutter();
   . . .
attr = {
        strokeOpacity: 0,
        x: item.get('column') * rectWidth,
        y: (item.get('row') - 1) * rectWidth,
        z: z,
. . .
. . .
attr = {
        strokeOpacity: 0,
        x: (item['column'] + 3) * rectWidth,
        y: (item['row']*(8 + i)) * rectWidth,
        z: z,
. . .
. . .
```

3. Update the `getDefaultSpriteConfig` method of the series class to use `elSize` to draw the element square:

```
getDefaultSpriteConfig: function() {
   return {
        type: this.seriesType,
        width: this.getElSize(),
        height: this.getElSize()
```

```
        };
    }
```

4. We now move on to the `PeriodicTable` sprite class and modify the
    `placeLabels` method to calculate the following based on the rectangle size:

    °   The font size for atomic number, name, and symbol texts

    °   The y position of the atomic number, name, and symbol texts within
        the element square

```
placeLabels: function(surface, ctx, clip, rect, attr) {

    var zScale = 0.2, symScale = 0.3, nameScale = 0.18;

  surface.add({
    type: 'text',
    x: attr.x + 5,
    y: attr.y + attr.width * zScale,
    text: attr.z,
    fontSize: attr.width * zScale,
    fillStyle: 'white'
  });

  surface.add({
    type: 'text',
    x: attr.x + 25,
    y: attr.y + attr.width * (zScale + symScale),
    text: attr.symbol,
    textAlign: 'center',
    fontSize: attr.width * symScale,
    fillStyle: 'white'
  });

  surface.add({
      type: 'text',
      x: attr.x + 5,
      y: attr.y + attr.width*(1 - nameScale),
      text: attr.name,
      fontSize: attr.width * nameScale,
      fillStyle: 'white'
  });

}
```

The zScale, symScale, and nameScale values have been determined statistically to derive the font size for atomic number, symbol, and name, respectively.

Try running the application with different values of elSize and you will see the texts scaling up/down, accordingly, as shown in the following screenshot:

But wait! What about the chart dimension and using it to calculate elSize?

Spacefilling chart supports the height and width configuration, which we can pass to our periodictable chart instance in the Main class. Now, based on these configurations, we will derive the value for elSize inside the series. We will make the following highlighted code changes to the getSprites series' method to derive the elSize value:

```
    . . .
        chart = me.getChart(),
        i, j, ln, ln1;

    var size = Math.max(chart.height, chart.width);
    var elSize = me.getElSize();

    if (size) {
        elSize = (size - (17*me.getGutter()))/18;
        me.setElSize(elSize);
    }

    var rectWidth = elSize + me.getGutter();

    // The store must be initialized
    if (!store) {
    . . .
    . . .
```

Now, you can control the element size by passing height and width to the chart. For brevity, we used the height or width, whichever is larger, in the calculation. The 18 is the number of columns that we have in a periodic table.

We had to set elSize on the series, as getDefaultSpriteConfig needs the calculated value.

As an exercise, you can try to refine the calculation to show the symbol in the center.

This brings us to the end of our discussion about how to create a custom spacefilling chart and how to handle certain important aspects to create data-driven, well-styled charts.

Summary

In this chapter, we discussed how to create a custom spacefilling chart where we created a series to create a periodic table and used that series with Sencha's spacefilling chart. We also discussed how to handle changing store data, styling sprites, and scaling up/down different dimensions. The implementation demonstrated Sencha Charts' important classes, their responsibilities, interactions, and how you can create a custom chart.

Now that we are done with creating different types of custom charts, in the next chapter, we will see how we can style and theme the charts.

7
Theming

We have created different types of charts. However, we did not do much about their styling—the fonts, color, background, animation, and so on. Styling is an important aspect of chart development and integrating charts into an application so that their look and feel gels with the overall application's look and feel. This chapter will focus solely on that aspect. In this chapter, we will cover the following topics:

- Styling a chart and its background
- Styling axes
- Styling different types of series
- Styling markers
- Styling legends
- Styling tooltips
- Styling labels

Sencha Charts offers three different mechanisms to style different aspects of a chart:

- Using configs
- Using a custom chart theme
- Using SASS

We will look at each one of these in detail to understand how we can offer a great looking chart to our users.

Getting ready

Check out the code from the GitHub repository and ensure that you see the following files in the ch07/app/view/main folder:

- Cartesian.js: This has the cartesian chart-related code and its style-related code.

- Polar.js: This has the polar chart with the radar series and its style-related code.

- Pie.js: This has the polar chart with the pie series and contains the pie series-specific styling code.

- ch07/app.js: This contains the following line, which you will have to modify to try different classes, mentioned above:

```
autoCreateViewport: 'SCE.view.main.Cartesian'
```

Styling using configs

The first mechanism to style different aspects of a chart is using the various configurations available on different Sencha Charts classes. Let's review them one by one.

Chart

The AbstractChart class is the base class for different types of charts. This class offers various configurations that we can use to style a chart. In this section, we will look at the chart level configurations and you will learn how to style different aspects of a chart.

Framing

To create a nice frame around the chart, we can use the shadow config. The only thing that we have to take note of is that it can be used only if the chart is a floating component. So, once we set up the following configuration on our cartesian chart, we have to additionally pass the height, width, and autoShow properties:

```
...
title: 'Chart',

height: 500,
width: 500,
```

```
autoShow: true,

floating: true,
shadow: true,
...
```

This is done as it is a floating component and does not have a parent container, and hence whether it needs to be shown or not and its dimensions must be explicitly specified.

By default, the `shadow` config is shown on the bottom-right corner. However, we want to frame the chart with shadow on all the sides. To achieve this, we will have to set the `shadow` attribute to `frame`. The possible values that the framework supports are as follows:

- `sides`: This shows the shadow on both the sides and the bottom.
- `frame`: This shows the shadow on all the sides.
- `drop`: This shows the shadow on the bottom-right corner. This is the default value.

The following screenshot shows the default shadow on the left-hand side and `frame` on the right-hand side:

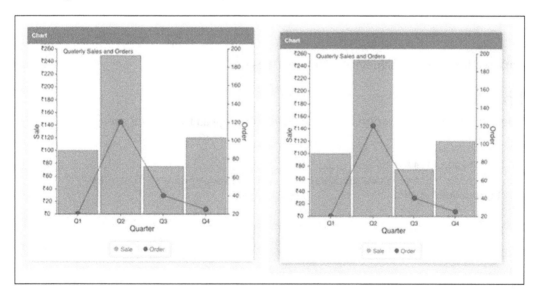

Coloring the background

By default, every chart has a white background. However, the chart surface does allow us to render the following as a chart background:

- Image
- Gradient
- Color

The background of a chart can be specified using the `background` config on a chart. The following screenshot shows the chart with three different types of backgrounds:

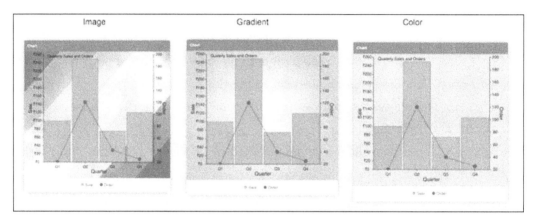

Let's see how we can achieve each one of these.

Image

The following configuration will let us use an image as the chart's background:

```
background: {
    type: 'image',
    src: 'http://www.psdgraphics.com/file/energy-efficiency-
background.jpg'
}
```

Gradient

To use a color gradient, the `background` value must be a valid
`Ext.draw.gradient.Linear` or `Ext.draw.gradient.Radial` object. Here is a
`radial` gradient that creates the background as shown in the previous screenshot,
under the heading **Gradient**:

```
background: {
    type: 'radial',
    start: {
        x: 0,
        y: 0,
        r: 0
    },
    end: {
        x: 0,
        y: 0,
        r: 1
    },
    stops: [
        {
         offset: 0,
         color: 'white'
        },
        {
         offset: 1,
         color: 'orange'
        }
    ]
}
```

Similarly, you can use a `linear` gradient.

Color

To use a single color as the chart's background, we have to set the color's HEX code
or name as the value for the `background` config, as shown here:

```
background: 'pink'
```

Changing the color of the series

The `AbstractChart` class defines a default set of colors and uses it to color the different series. However, this can be modified by specifying the `colors` config on the chart. Consider the following configuration:

```
colors: ['pink', '#60D5DB']
```

- This configuration will color the series as shown here:

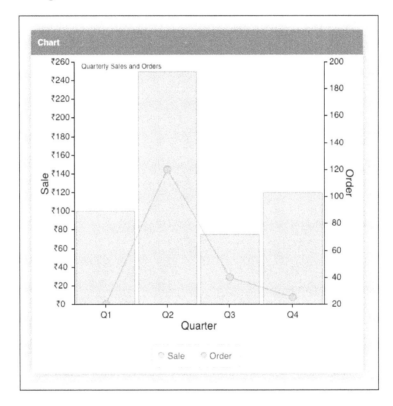

The `colors` array must contain an entry for each series that is added to the chart and a series index is used to find its color.

 A series will not be visible if there is no color defined for its index in the `colors` array.

Creating room at the sides

In our chart, we have a chart title on the top—**Quarterly Sales and Orders**—which is overlapping with the **Sales** axis. So, we will create room for the title by adding padding to our chart. The special config—insetPadding—will help us achieve this. The following configuration on the chart will create a 40px padding from all the sides of the chart:

```
insetPadding: 40
```

The following screenshot shows the output without and with insetPadding:

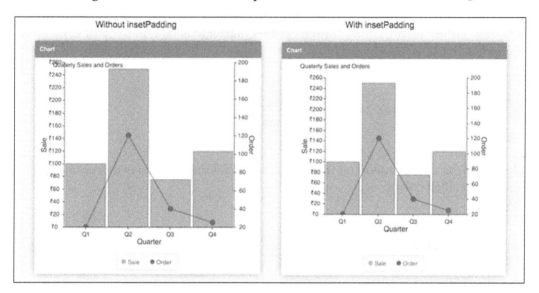

To add different padding values to different sides, we can pass the side-specific values as shown here:

```
insetPadding: {
    top: 40,
    left: 20,
    bottom: 5,
    right: 5
}
```

 The chart-level configurations are common to all types of charts—cartesian, polar, and spacefilling.

Axis

The axis is applicable to all cartesian charts and some polar charts, such as radar. We will see what kind of styling can be done using the axis-level configuration.

Displaying grid lines

To draw the basic grid lines, we will have to set the `grid` property to `true` on the required axis. For example, the following screenshot shows grid lines configured on the **Sale** and **Quarter** axes.

We can use different colors to draw a grid by setting some advanced configurations for `grid`. The following configuration on the **Quarter** axis will fill the odd rows with the #999 color:

```
grid: {
    odd: {
        fillStyle: '#999'
    }
}
```

The following configuration on the **Sale** axis will fill the odd and even columns as per the specified colors:

```
grid: {
    odd: {
        fillStyle: 'yellow'
    },
    even: {
        fillStyle: 'cyan'
    },
    opacity: 0.7
}
```

We set the `opacity` level so that the color of the grid row of the **Quarter** axis grid can also be seen.

The following screenshot shows the results produced with the basic and advanced grid configurations:

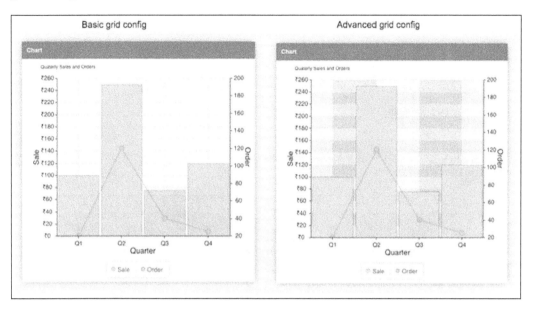

Axes grids are rendered in the order in which the axes are listed in the axes configuration of a chart. So, you will have to order them based on how you want to see the grid's row/column colors.

Styling an axis line

The `style` configuration on an axis provides the capability to style the axis line. The `style` object must have the attributes listed in the `Ext.chart.axis.sprite.Axis` class. For example, the following configuration on the **Sale** axis hides the axis line but renders the ticks in red color with 2px width:

```
style: {
    strokeStyle: 'red',
    lineWidth: 2,
    axisLine: false
}
```

Styling axis labels

Axis labels can be customized using the `label` config. The following configuration on the **Order** axis will style the **Order** labels in red color and will rotate them by the mentioned degree:

```
label: {
    fontSize: 14,
    color: 'red',
    rotationRads: -45
}
```

Similarly, the `label` style can be configured on the **Quarter** axis as well. Here is how the output looks like:

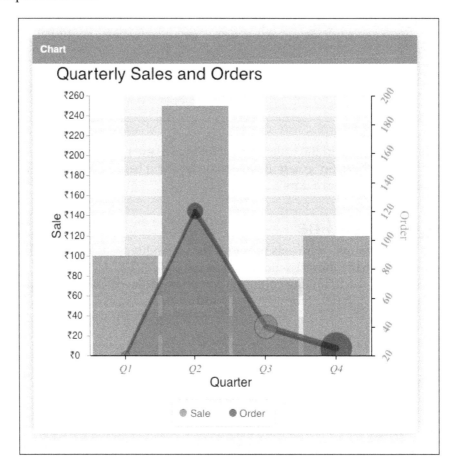

Displaying a custom label

It would be good if the value labels on the **Sale** axis can also show the currency symbol. To achieve this, we can implement the `renderer` method on the **Sale** axis and return the label with the INR currency symbol, as shown here:

```
renderer: function(label, layout, lastLabel) {
    return '₹' + label;
}
```

The following screenshot shows the **Sale** axis labels without and with `renderer`:

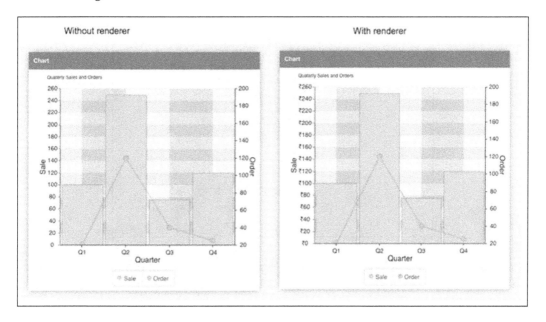

Axis-related styling is applicable, primarily, to the cartesian charts. However, radar, which is a polar chart, also requires the axes configuration and is available for styling. The following screenshot shows a radar styled using the preceding configs:

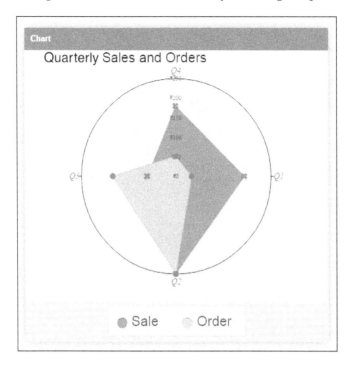

A spacefilling chart does not have an axis. So, these configs will not have any effect on it.

Series

Like charts and axis, series also offer certain configurations to style them. We will discuss these configurations in the following sections.

Animating a series

To animate a series, we need to set the `animation` config on the series. The value can either be `true` or an `Ext.fx.Anim` object. If it is set to `true`, the framework uses `ease` as the default animation for a duration of 250 milliseconds. We can use a different animation by passing an `animation` object, as shown here:

```
animation: {
    easing: 'elasticIn',
```

```
        duration: 1000
    }
```

This config is not applicable to all the different types of series. For example, Radar does not use this, whereas a pie series does.

Using our own color

A series also offers the `colors` config where we can indicate the color for that series. Why colors? When do we have to pass an array of color codes? The answer is, if a series shows multiple sprites, for example, a stacked bar series showing two data samples, it will use the `colors` array to find out the color for a sprite corresponding to a data sample.

The `colors` array on the chart designates color to each series. However, the `colors` array on a series designates color to the different sprites that it draws for each data sample.

Highlighting

A series supports highlighting where it can change its sprite style on mouseover. It is driven based on the `highlight` configuration. Value for `highlight` can either be `true` or the `Ext.draw.sprite.Sprite` object. If the value is set to `true`, the series class uses the `highlightCfg` config to highlight a series sprite. If an object is specified, it is merged with `highlightCfg` and the effective attributes are applied to the sprite. In case the same config is specified in `highlightCfg` as well as `highlight`, the `highlight` config takes higher priority and would be effective. For example, the following `highlight` configuration on bar series highlights the bar sprite with a shadow and shifts its *y* coordinate by `5px`:

```
highlight: {
    strokeStyle: '#094144',
    fillStyle: '#60D5DB',
    shadowColor: "#999",
    shadowOffsetX: 5,
    shadowOffsetY: 5,
    translationY: 5
}
```

The following screenshot shows the highlighted bar based on the previous configuration:

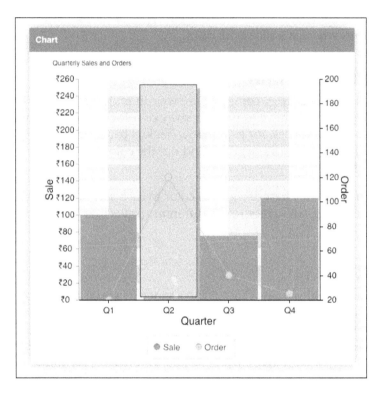

Again, highlighting behavior will not be the same, or sometimes unavailable for some types of series. For example, radar does not have it, whereas pie does. Bar highlights the bar, whereas line highlights the marker, if anything at all.

Styling a series sprite

A series sprite can be styled using the following configurations:

- `style`: This is applied to the series sprite. This overrides the style provided by the theme.
- `subStyle`: This is applied in a cyclic fashion if there are multiple sprites in a series. For example, a bar series with multiple bars (for multiple data samples).

If the same style-related attribute is defined in `style` as well as `subStyle`, for example, `fillStyle`, the `subStyle` config takes precedence.

The chart framework derives a darker version of sprite color based on its `fillStyle` config to draw the sprite outline. To disable this, we can set `useDarkerStrokeColor` to `false`.

Styling the marker

The `markerSubStyle` config is available to provide the styling for a series marker. This must be configured on a series. For example, consider the following configuration:

```
markerSubStyle: {
    fillStyle: 'green',
    radius: 15,
    shadowColor: "pink",
    shadowOffsetX: 2,
    shadowOffsetY: 2
}
```

This configuration styles the `circle` marker, as shown here:

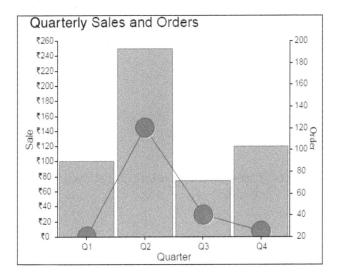

A marker can be styled based on `gradients` defined at the chart level. Each item in the gradients array is of type – `Ext.draw.gradient.Gradient`. Sent Charts has defined two subclasses of it – `Radial` and `Linear` – which can be used to implement color gradients. For example, say, we have the following `gradients` configured on the cartesian chart:

```
gradients: [{
    id: 'gradientId1',
    type: 'linear',
```

```
        angle: 45,
        stops: [{
            offset: 0,
            color: 'white'
        }, {
            offset: 1,
            color: 'orange'
        }]
    }, {
        id: 'gradientId2',
        type: 'radial',
        stops: [{
            offset: 0,
            color: 'white',
        }, {
            offset: 1,
            color: 'orange',
        }]
    }]
```

Now, we can use this to style the circle marker by configuring the following on the line series:

```
marker: {
    radius: 15,
    fillStyle: 'url(#gradientId1)',
    strokeStyle: 'url(#gradientId2)'
}
```

This will style the markers based on the gradients, as shown here:

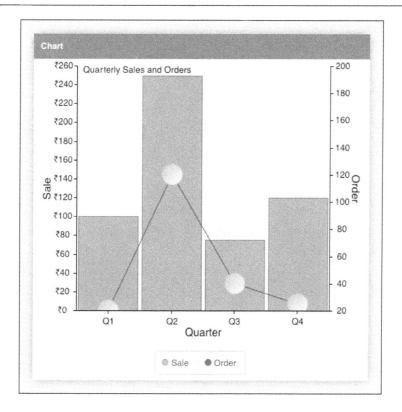

Usage of gradients is not limited to styling the markers. They can be used with style, subStyle, and markerSubStyle configs as well.

A marker can also be styled using the renderer config, which we will see next.

Customizing the rendering logic

The renderer config is available on a series and using this, we can implement custom logic to style the series sprite, including markers. For example, the following renderer config on the line series will style the marker and the line stroke based on its custom logic:

```
renderer: function(sprite, config, rendererData, index) {
    if (config.type === 'marker') {
        return {
            fillStyle: (index % 2 === 0 ? 'red' : 'black'),
```

```
            radius: (index + 1) * 5
        };
    }

    if (config.type === 'line') {
        return {
            lineWidth: (index + 1) * 2,
            lineJoin: 'round'
        }
    }

}
```

The preceding config will style the marker and the line stroke as shown in the following screenshot:

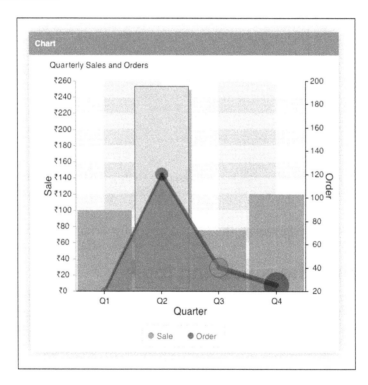

A radar series does not use the `renderer` config unlike the Pie and Pie3D series. Here is the output of a custom `renderer` config for the Pie series that can create pies with the radius based on the order to sales ratio:

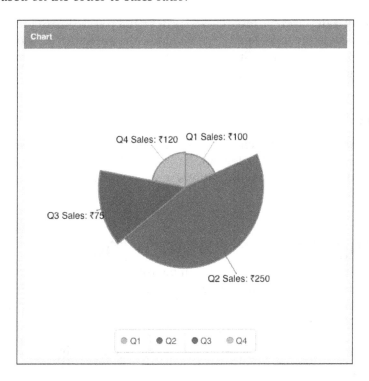

The `renderer` config calculates `endRho` for a pie/sector sprite for each quarter, based on that quarter's sales and order, as shown here:

```
renderer: function(sprite, config, rendererData, index) {
    var sales = rendererData.store.getData().items[index].
get('sales');
    var order = rendererData.store.getData().items[index].
get('order');

    return {
        strokeStyle: 'red',
        lineWidth: 2,
        label: sprite.attr.label + ' Sales: ₹' + sales,
        endRho: sprite.attr.endRho * order/sales * 1.5
    }
}
```

Sprite

A sprite can be directly added to a chart using its `sprites` configuration.
For example, we have added a `text` type sprite to our chart to show the chart
title — **Quarterly Sales and Orders**. These sprites can be styled using their attributes.
For example, to style the `text` sprite, we must use the attributes defined by the
`Ext.draw.sprite.Text` class. Similarly, to style a `circle` sprite, we must use the
attributes defined by the `Ext.draw.sprite.Circle` class.

Legend

A legend is a container component that uses a data view. There is no specific styling
configuration available to style a legend. It relies on the component's style and
CSS-related configs, which we will visit when we look at the *Theming using SASS
and CSS* section.

Theming using a custom theme

A chart provides a `theme` config, which can be used to associate a chart theme to it.
A chart theme is a subclass of the `Ext.chart.theme.Base` class. The framework
offers various subclasses, which can be used to style our chart. These classes are
located under the `ext/packages/sencha-charts/src/chart/theme` folder.

For example, we can use the `PurpleGradients` class and configure `theme` on the
cartesian and pie chart with an alias name — `purple-gradients`:

```
theme: 'purple-gradients'
```

The theme produces the following results:

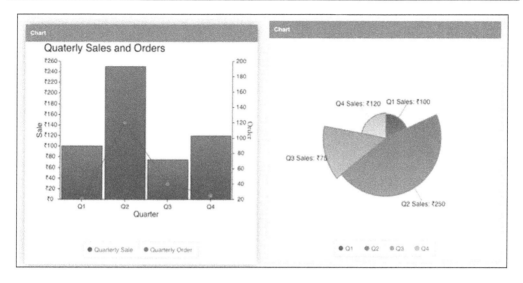

Similarly, we can try other existing themes to see which one suits our requirements.

However, none of them are close to our need, as before we had a custom background image and a series rendered in different colors. Also, the labels need to be styled differently for the axes. So, we have to define our own custom theme. Here is definition of our custom theme, `awesome`:

```
Ext.define('SCE.view.chart.theme.Awesome', {
    extend: 'Ext.chart.theme.Base',
    singleton: true,
    alias: 'chart.theme.awesome',

    config: {
        colors: ['#6F5092', '#64BD4F'],
        gradients: {
          type: 'linear',
          degrees:90
      },
    chart: {
        defaults: {
            background: 'pink'
        },
        cartesian: {
          background: {
                    type: 'image',
                    src: ' resources/images/energy-efficiency-
background.jpg'
```

```
                        }
                    }
                },
                series: {
                    defaults: {
                        style: {
                            lineWidth: 2
                        }
                    },
                    bar: {
                        animation: {
                            easing: 'bounceIn',
                            duration: 1000
                        }
                    },
                    line: {
                        style: {
                            strokeStyle: '#00904B'
                        }
                    }
                },
                axis: {
                    defaults: {
                        style: {strokeStyle: 'red'}
                    },
                    left: {
                        grid: {
                            odd: {
                                fillStyle: 'yellow'
                            },
                            even: {
                                fillStyle: 'cyan'
                            },
                            opacity: 0.7
                        },
                        title: {fillStyle: '#6F5092', fontSize: 'default*1.5'},
                        label: {fillStyle: '#6F5092', fontSize: 'default*1.5'}
                    },
                    right: {
                        title: {fillStyle: '#00904B'},
                        label: {fillStyle: '#00904B', rotationRads: -45}
                    },
                    bottom: {
                        grid: {
```

```
                    odd: {
                        fillStyle: '#999'
                    }
                }
            }
        }
    }
});
```

As part of the chart definition, the `defaults` configuration applies to all types of charts, whereas `cartesian` applies only to the cartesian chart. The chart `xtype` name must be used to define the chart-specific override. For example, for a cartesian chart, `background` is overridden to use an image, whereas for polar and Spacefilling charts, pink color will be used as their background.

To define styles for series, sprites and axes, we will have to configure `series`, `sprites`, and `axis`, respectively.

 You can refer to the `Ext.chart.theme.Base` class to find out the complete list of theme-related configurations.

The following screenshot shows how the chart would look like with our custom theme:

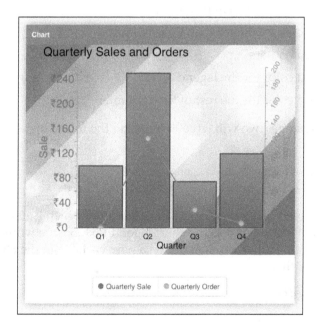

The class is available in the `ch07/app/view/chart/theme` folder.

Theming using SASS and CSS

Sencha Charts does not offer much in terms of styling charts, axes, series, sprites, and markers using SASS and CSS. This is not a problem because the Canvas drawings cannot be styled using CSS as they are not rendered as DOM elements. However, SVG is rendered as a DOM element and it is possible to style them with CSS. However, to make the APIs look and behave consistently across SVG and Canvas, the framework offers class-level configurations and derives the styles based on their values, which we saw in the earlier sections.

Having mentioned that there is one part of the chart that can be styled using CSS. The `ext/packages/sencha-charts/sass` folder defines SASS variables and theming code related to the legend. So, in order to modify the legend style, we will have to work with them.

Let's say, we want our legend to look like this:

We will change the following settings:

- Legend text is bigger than its default
- Colored circles are bigger than their default
- No rounded corners
- Background color for the legend area
- Background color for the rest of the container

To achieve these changes, we will have to override the following existing SASS variables:

```
$chart-legend-border-radius: 0px !default;
$chart-legend-item-background: #FBEFF2 !default;
```

The text size is derived using the `$font-size` variable, which is used across the framework. It is not just limited to the chart legend text. So, we would not like to override `$font-size`. Rather, we will define a new variable in the `ch07/sass/var/Application.scss` file:

```
$chart-legend-font-size: 22px !default;
```

Since we have defined a new variable, we will have to modify the style code, which is in the `src/chart/AbstractChart.scss` file, to use this new variable. We will define the following style in the `ch07/sass/src/Application.scss` file:

```
.#{$prefix}legend-item {
  background: $chart-legend-item-background;
  font-size: $chart-legend-font-size;
}
```

Additionally, to set the background color for the legend container, we will set the following CSS:

```
.x-legend, .x-legend-panel .x-panel-body {
  background: #DCDCDC;
}
```

Now, we will create the CSS from the SASS mentioned earlier. To do this, you may perform an application build or try other Sencha Cmd commands, such as `application watch`, to compile SASS and create CSS.

Refresh the application and we can see that the legend area has been styled as expected, as shown here:

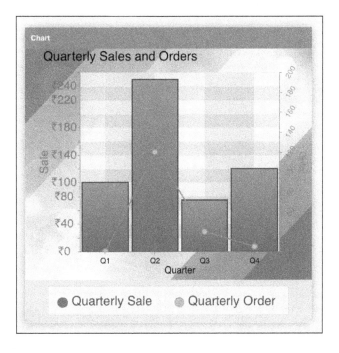

This ends our discussion on theming charts created using Sencha Charts.

Summary

In this chapter, you learned about the different ways to style different aspects of a chart—background, axes, series, sprites, markers, and labels. We saw how we can create great-looking charts using the configurations or by defining a custom chart theme or using SASS and CSS.

In the next chapter, we will talk about building interactivity into the charts where users can interact with them to get more information out of them.

8
Working with Touch Gestures

Gestures are a powerful nonverbal mode of communication where we communicate the meaning or idea using body parts, such as hands and face. In computers, different devices offer different gestures, which are typically a combination of one or more events originating from a DOM element. We have hand gestures such as, pinch, drag, swipe, and so on, available on touch devices. Sencha Charts uses them to offer interactions for their charts and makes visual analysis possible. With the help of interactions, one can mark a specific section of a chart, leave a note, zoom into it, and so on.

In this chapter, we will cover:

- Touch gestures support in Sencha Charts
- Using gestures on existing charts
- Out-of-the-box interactions
- Creating custom interactions using touch gestures
- Applying custom interactions to an existing chart
- Applying custom interactions to custom charts

Interacting with interactions

The interactions code is located under the `ext/packages/sencha-charts/src/chart/interactions` folder. The `Ext.chart.interactions.Abstract` class is the base class for all the chart interactions.

Interactions must be associated with a chart by configuring `interactions` on it. Consider the following example:

```
Ext.create('Ext.chart.PolarChart', {
    title: 'Chart',
    interactions: ['rotate'],
    ...
```

The `gestures` config is an important config. It is an integral part of an interaction where it tells the framework which touch gestures would be part of an interaction. It's a map where the event name is the key and the `handler` method name is its value. Consider the following example:

```
gestures: {
    tap: 'onTapGesture',
    doubletap: 'onDoubleTapGesture'
}
```

Once an interaction has been associated with a chart, the framework registers the events and their handlers, as listed in the `gestures` config, on the chart as part of the chart initialization, as shown here:

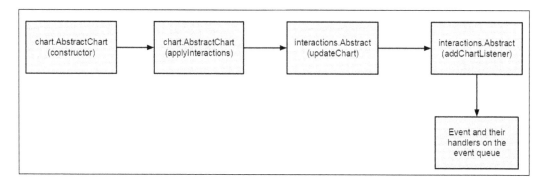

Here is what happens during each stage of the preceding flowchart:

1. The chart's construction starts when its constructor is called either by a call to `Ext.create` or `xtype` usage.

2. The `interactions` config is applied to the `AbstractChart` class by the class system, which calls the `applyInteractions` method.

3. The `applyInteractions` method sets the chart object on each of the interaction objects. This setter operation will call the `updateChart` method of the interaction class—`Ext.chart.interactions.Abstract`.

4. The `updateChart` calls `addChartListener` to add the gesture-related events and their handlers.

5. The `addChartListener` iterates through the `gestures` object and registers the listed events and their handlers on the chart object.

> Interactions work on touch as well as non-touch devices (for example, desktop). On non-touch devices, the gestures are simulated based on their mouse or pointer events. For example, `mousedown` is treated as a `tap` event.

Using built-in interactions

Here is a list of the built-in interactions:

- **Crosshair**: This interaction helps the user to get precise x and y values for a specific point on a chart. Because of this, it is applicable to cartesian charts only. The x and y values are obtained by single-touch dragging on the chart.

  The interaction also offers additional configs:

  ○ axes: This can be used to provide label text and label rectangle configs on a per axis basis using `left`, `right`, `top`, and `bottom` configs or a single config applying to all the axes. If the axes config is not specified, the axis label value is shown as the text and the rectangle will be filled with white color.

  ○ lines: The interaction draws horizontal and vertical lines through the point on the chart. Line sprite attributes can be passed using horizontal or vertical configs.

For example, we configure the following `crosshair` interaction on a CandleStick chart:

```
interactions: [{
    type: 'crosshair',
    axes: {
        left: {
            label: { fillStyle: 'white' },
            rect: {
                fillStyle: 'pink',
                radius: 2
            }
        },
        bottom: {
            label: {
                fontSize: '14px',
                fontWeight: 'bold'
            },
            rect: { fillStyle: 'cyan' }
        }
    }
}]
```

The preceding configuration will produce the following output, where the labels and rectangles on the two axes have been styled as per the configuration:

- **CrossZoom**: This interaction allows the user to zoom in on a selected area of a chart using drag events. It is very useful in getting the microscopic view of your macroscopic data view. For example, the chart presents month-wise data for two years; using zoom, you can look at the values for, say, a specific month. The interaction offers an additional config – axes – using which we indicate the axes, which will be zoomed. Consider the following configuration on a CandleStick chart:

```
interactions: [{
    type: 'crosszoom',
    axes: ['left', 'bottom']
}]
```

This will produce the following output where a user will be able to zoom in to both the `left` and `bottom` axes:

Additionally, we can control the zoom level by passing `minZoom` and `maxZoom`, as shown in the following snippet:

```
interactions: [{
    type: 'crosszoom',
    axes: {
        left: {
            maxZoom: 8,
            startZoom: 2
        },
        bottom: true
    }
}]
```

The zoom is reset when the user double-clicks on the chart.

- **ItemHighlight**: This interaction allows the user to highlight series items in the chart. It works in conjunction with `highlight` config that is configured on a series. The interaction identifies and sets the `highlightItem` on a chart, on which the `highlight` and `highlightCfg` configs are applied. You can refer to the *Highlighting* section of *Chapter 7*, *Theming*, for more details.

- **PanZoom**: This interaction allows the user to navigate the data for one or more chart axes by panning and/or zooming. Navigation can be limited to particular axes.

  Pinch gestures are used for zooming whereas drag gestures are used for panning. For devices which do not support multiple-touch events, zooming cannot be done via pinch gestures; in this case, the interaction will allow the user to perform both zooming and panning using the same single-touch drag gesture.

  By default, zooming is not enabled. We can enable it by setting `zoomOnPanGesture:true` on the interaction, as shown here:

  ```
  interactions: {
      type: 'panzoom',
      zoomOnPanGesture: true
  }
  ```

  By default, all the axes are navigable. However, the panning and zooming can be controlled at axis level, as shown here:

  ```
  {
      type: 'panzoom',
      axes: {
          left: {
              maxZoom: 5,
              allowPan: false
          },
          bottom: true
      }
  }
  ```

- **Rotate**: This interaction allows the user to rotate a polar chart about its center. It implements the rotation using the single-touch drag gestures.

  This interaction does not have any additional config.

- **RotatePie3D**: This is an extension of the `Rotate` interaction to rotate a Pie3D chart. This does not have any additional config.

  In the following section, we will create some custom interactions and use them on existing charts of Sencha Charts and the custom charts that we created in *Chapter 4, Creating a Custom Cartesian Chart; Chapter 5, Creating a Custom Polar Chart;* and *Chapter 6, Creating a Custom Spacefilling Chart.*

Creating custom interactions

In this section, we will create three different interactions:

- **Trendline**: This allows the user to draw straight lines on a cartesian chart. It is a completely custom-developed interaction class and we will see how it can be used with an existing CandleStick as well as a custom MACD chart that we developed in *Chapter 4, Creating a Custom Cartesian Chart.*

- **Annotation**: This allows the user to annotate a chart by adding an annotation image with a text. This will be a custom interaction, which we will use with our custom MarketClock chart that we developed in *Chapter 5, Creating a Custom Polar Chart.*

- **ItemHighlight**: This is a custom interaction. It allows the user to show more details about a selected series item. We will leverage the Sencha Charts architecture, modify an existing interaction, and use it on our custom PeriodicTable chart that we developed in *Chapter 6, Creating a Custom Spacefilling Chart.*

Each of these three interactions will explain unique scenarios that we might come across during any interaction development and use it on different types of charts.

Displaying a trend line

A trend line is a great analysis tool to find out the upward or downward trend of a script.

 You can read more about trend line and its application at `http://en.wikipedia.org/wiki/Trend_line_(technical_analysis)`.

In *Chapter 4, Creating a Custom Cartesian Chart*, we created a CandleStick chart along with a MACD indicator. Now, we will add support for drawing any number of trend lines on the CandleStick as well as MACD charts to be able to analyze the trend, as shown in the following screenshot:

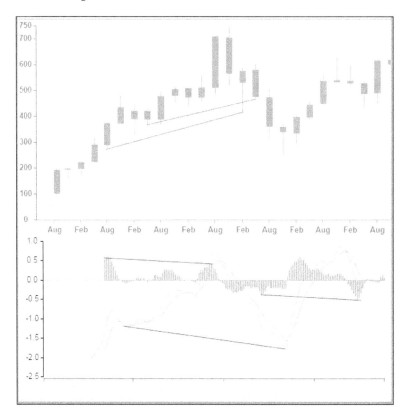

In the preceding screenshot, we have drawn trend lines on the CandleStick in red color, whereas on MACD, it is in purple. Say, we consider the following as requirements for our Trend Line interaction:

- Trend line should work only for a cartesian chart
- We can draw any number of trend lines on a chart
- Trend line attributes will be configurable
- Trend line will work with out-of-the-box cartesian charts

The following steps define the new interaction and use it on different charts:

1. Copy the ch04 folder's contents to the ch08/ch08_01 folder.
2. Go to the ch08/ch08_01 folder.
3. Create a Trendline.js file under the app/interactions folder and save the following code in it:

```
Ext.define('SCE.interactions.Trendline', {

    extend: 'Ext.chart.interactions.Abstract',
    requires: [
        'Ext.chart.CartesianChart'
    ],

    type: 'trendline',
    alias: 'interaction.trendline',

    config: {
        line: {
            strokeStyle: 'red'
        },

        gesture: 'drag'
    },

    applyLine: function (lineConfig, oldLineConfig) {
        return Ext.merge(oldLineConfig || {}, lineConfig);
    },

    updateChart: function (chart) {
        if (!(chart instanceof Ext.chart.CartesianChart)) {
            throw 'Trendline interaction can only be used on
cartesian charts.';
        }
        this.callParent(arguments);
    },

    getGestures: function () {
        var me = this,
            gestures = {};
        gestures[me.getGesture() + 'start'] = 'onGestureStart';
        gestures[me.getGesture()] = 'onGesture';
```

```
        gestures[me.getGesture() + 'end'] = 'onGestureEnd';
        return gestures;
    },

    onGestureStart: function (e) {
        var me = this;

        var chart = me.getChart(),
            surface = chart.getSurface('overlay'),
            rect = chart.getInnerRect(),
            chartWidth = rect[2],
            chartHeight = rect[3],
            xy = chart.getEventXY(e),
            x = xy[0],
            y = xy[1],
            lineConfig = me.getLine();

        if (x > 0 && x < chartWidth && y > 0 && y < chartHeight) {
            me.lockEvents(me.getGesture());
            me.trendLine = surface.add(Ext.apply({
                xclass: 'Ext.draw.sprite.Line',
                fromX: x,
                fromY: y
            }, lineConfig));
        }

    },

    onGesture: function (e) {
        var me = this;
        if (me.getLocks()[me.getGesture()] !== me) {
            return;
        }
        var chart = me.getChart(),
            surface = chart.getSurface('overlay'),
            rect = Ext.Array.slice(chart.getInnerRect()),
            padding = chart.getInnerPadding(),
            px = padding.left,
            py = padding.top,
            chartWidth = rect[2],
            chartHeight = rect[3],
            xy = chart.getEventXY(e),
```

```
                x = xy[0],
                y = xy[1];

        if (x < 0) {
            x = 0;
        } else if (x > chartWidth) {
            x = chartWidth;
        }
        if (y < 0) {
            y = 0;
        } else if (y > chartHeight) {
            y = chartHeight;
        }
        x += px;
        y += py;

        me.trendLine.setAttributes({toX: x, toY: y});
        surface.renderFrame();
    },

    onGestureEnd: function (e) {
        var me = this,
            chart = me.getChart(),
            surface =  chart.getSurface('overlay');

        surface.renderFrame();
        me.unlockEvents(me.getGesture());
    }

});
```

In the preceding code, we defined our new interaction—trendline—using single-click and drag gestures. The getGestures method prepares the gestures array with the drag gesture events—dragstart, drag, and dragend—and their handlers.

A line is drawn on the overlay surface so that it appears on top of the series sprites.

The onGestureStart and onGestureEnd methods are called once, at the beginning and end of the drag gesture, respectively. The onGestureStart method creates a line sprite with its starting point set, and keeps it with the class that is used by the onGesture method. The onGesture method sets the ending point for the line sprite based on the current drag event coordinate. After the attributes are set on the line sprite, we need to call the renderFrame method on the overlay surface so that the sprite can be drawn on the canvas with the new attributes. This will ensure that the line is seen on the screen.

The onGestureStart method checks whether the event has originated within the chart area, and only then, it locks the event so that the gesture does not conflict with other interactions configured on the chart that use the same gesture. For example, if both panzoom and trendline interactions are configured on a CandleStick chart in the mentioned order, drag gesture will only pan/zoom the chart as it will first lock the gesture and trendline will not be drawn on the chart. This is because both interactions rely on the same drag gesture.

When we lock the gesture event, we must ensure that we unlock it when we are done, which we are doing in the onGestureEnd method as dragend marks the end of our interaction.

The onGesture method does not check to ensure that the trend line does not cross the chart area when the user drags beyond the chart area.

The interaction also offers an additional config — line — which allows us to style the trend line for a chart. This config is defaulted as follows:

```
{
    strokeStyle: 'red'
}
```

This means all the trend lines will be red in color unless a different strokeStyle is mentioned on a chart using the line config.

The applyLine method is called to apply the line config to the interaction. This method merges the line configuration passed to a chart with the default configuration.

The updateChart method is implemented to throw an exception if the associated chart is not a cartesian chart.

4. Edit the app/view/Main.js file and add the trendline interaction to the CandleStick and MACD charts, as highlighted here in bold:

```
{

        xtype: 'candlestick-test-chart',
        height: 350,
```

```
        interactions: ['trendline']
    },
    {

        xclass: 'SCE.chart.MACD',
        interactions: {
            type: 'trendline',
            line: {
                // lineDash: [5, 5],
                strokeStyle: 'purple'
            }
        },
    ...
```

In this code, we have set up the trend line with `purple` color on the MACD chart, whereas the CandleStick chart uses the default color, `red`.

5. Run the application inside your browser and you will be able to draw the trend lines on the CandleStick as well as MACD charts.

Annotating a chart

Annotation helps us to add more details or notes to our charts, which can be handy in the interpretation. We will create a new interaction—`Annotation`—which allows the user to add any number of annotations to the text, as shown here:

In the preceding screenshot, we have drawn two annotations, shown as images with **A** alphabet with their texts. We will consider the following as requirements for our Annotation interaction:

- Annotations should work with the MarketClock chart
- We can add any number of annotations on a chart with their own text
- We can edit the annotation text
- We can remove an annotation

The following steps define the new interaction and use it on the MarketClock chart:

1. Copy the `ch05` folder's contents to the `ch08/ch08_02` folder.
2. Go to the `ch08/ch08_02` folder.
3. Create a `Annotation.js` file under the `app/interactions` folder and save the following code in it:

```
Ext.define('SCE.interactions.Annotation', {

    extend: 'Ext.chart.interactions.Abstract',
    requires: [
        'Ext.window.MessageBox'
    ],

    type: 'annotation',
    alias: 'interaction.annotation',

    config: {
        addGesture: 'doubletap',
        editGesture: 'tap',

        events: [
            'annotationadded',
            'annotationremoved',
            'annotationupdated'
        ]
    },

    annotations: [],

    getGestures: function () {
        var me = this,
            gestures = {};
        gestures[me.getAddGesture()] = 'onAddGesture';
```

```
        gestures[me.getEditGesture()] = 'onEditGestureEnd';
        return gestures;
    },

onAddGesture: function (e) {
    var me = this,
        xy = me.getChartPosition(e),
        chart = me.getChart(),
        surface = chart.getSurface('overlay');

    //show an image to indicate annotation
    var img = {
            type: 'image',
            x: xy[0] - 15,
            y: xy[1] - 30,
            draggable: true,
            src: 'resources/images/Annotation.png'
    };

    var item = surface.add(img);
    surface.renderFrame();

    //create a dialog with text area
    Ext.Msg.show({
        header:false,
        buttons: Ext.Msg.YESNOCANCEL,
        buttonText: {yes: 'Save', no: 'Remove'},
        multiline: true,
        closable: false,
        fn: function( btn , text, opt){
            if (btn == 'no') {
                //remove the annotation sprite
                surface.remove(item);
                surface.renderFrame();

                chart.fireEvent('annotationremoved', chart,
e);
            } else {
                //yes and cancel button
                //set the annotation text and add annotation
to the internal cache
```

```
                          me.annotations.push({text: text, sprite:
item});

                        chart.fireEvent('annotationadded', chart,
text, item, e);
                }
            }
        });
    },

    onEditGestureEnd: function(e) {
        var me = this,
            chart = me.getChart(),
            surface = chart.getSurface('overlay'),
            item = me.getMatchingAnnotationSprite(e);

        if (item) {
            //create a dialog with text area populated for edit
            Ext.Msg.show({
                header:false,
                buttons: Ext.Msg.YESNOCANCEL,
                buttonText: {yes: 'Save', no: 'Remove'},
                multiline: true,
                closable: false,
                value: item.text,
                fn: function( btn , text, opt){
                    if( btn == 'cancel' ){
                        //do nothing, for now
                    } else if (btn == 'no') {
                        //remove the annotation sprite
                        surface.remove(item.sprite);
                        surface.renderFrame();

                        chart.fireEvent('annotationremoved',
chart, e);
                    } else {
                        //yes button
                        //set the annotation text and add
annotation to the internal cache
                        var oldTxt = item.text;
                        item.text = text;
                        chart.fireEvent('annotationupdated',
chart, item.text, oldTxt, item.sprite, e);
```

```
                    }
                }
            });
        }
    },

    getChartPosition: function(e) {
        var me = this;

        var chart = me.getChart(),
            surface = chart.getSurface('overlay'),
            rect = chart.getMainRect(),              chartWidth =
rect[2],
            chartHeight = rect[3],
            xy = chart.getEventXY(e),
            x = xy[0],
            y = xy[1];

        if (x < 0) {
            x = 0;
        } else if (x > chartWidth) {
            x = chartWidth;
        }
        if (y < 0) {
            y = 0;
        } else if (y > chartHeight) {
            y = chartHeight;
        }

        return [x, y];
    },

    getMatchingAnnotationSprite: function(e) {
        var me = this;
        var tmp = null,
            items = me.annotations,
            i,
            l = items.length,
            xy = me.getChartPosition(e),
            x = xy[0],
            y = xy[1];

        for (i = 0; i < l; i++) {
```

```
                    tmp = items[i];

                    var attr = tmp.sprite.attr;

                    if ((x >= attr.x && x <= (attr.x + 30)) &&
                        (y >= attr.y && y <= (attr.y + 30))) {
                        return tmp;
                    }
                }
            }
        }

});
```

The preceding code defines our annotation interaction, which allows us to perform the following tasks:

- Add a new annotation using `doubletap`. When the event is fired, the interaction draws a 30x30 pixels `image` sprite to display the annotation and brings up the message popup to allow the user to enter the annotation text.

- Edit/update the existing annotation using `tap`. When the tap event is fired, based on the event coordinates, it locates the annotation at that position by calling the `getMatchingAnnotationSprite` method, and if one exists, it brings up the popup message box to edit the already entered text.

The annotation images are added to the `overlay` surface and hence they will appear on top of the series sprites.

The interaction also fires three events:

- `annotationadded`: This is fired when a new annotation is added to a chart by clicking on the **Save** button on the popup message box.

- `annotationremoved`: This is fired when an existing annotation is removed. A user can remove an annotation by clicking on the **Remove** button on the popup message box.

- `annotationupdated`: This is fired when the text of an existing annotation is updated by clicking on the **Save** button on the popup message box.

You can register handlers for the preceding events to drive further application behavior.

The `getChartPosition` method is a private method that normalizes the event coordinates if they exceed the chart boundary.

4. Edit the `app/view/Main.js` file and add the `annotation` interaction to the MarketClock chart, as highlighted here in bold:

```
items: [{
    xtype: 'marketclock',
    interactions: ['annotation'],
    ...
```

5. Run the application inside your browser and you will be able to add any number of annotations to the MarketClock.

Displaying more details of a series item

Let's pick up our PeriodicTable chart and, say, we want to add an interaction to the chart so that we can identify the element that has been clicked/tapped and use the selected element's information to show more details about it, as shown here:

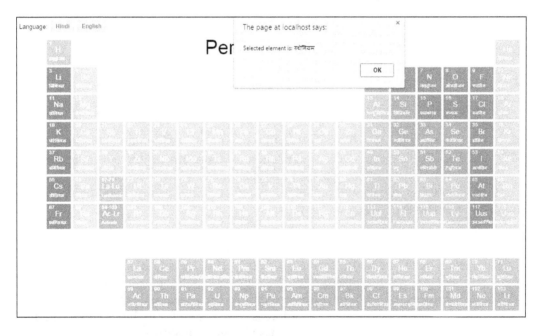

In this screenshot, we have shown the selected element's name in an alert. This can be enhanced to show more details about the selected element, say, to show a popup window with the details of the element from Wikipedia. However, I will leave that as an exercise for you.

The following steps define the new interaction and use it on the PeriodicTable chart:

1. Copy the ch06 folder's contents to the ch08/ch08_03 folder.

2. Go to the ch08/ch08_03 folder.

3. Create a ItemHighlight.js file under the app/interactions folder and save the following code in it:

```
Ext.define('SCE.interactions.ItemHighlight', {

    extend: 'Ext.chart.interactions.ItemHighlight',

    type: 'sce-itemhighlight',
    alias: 'interaction.sce-itemhighlight',

    gestures: {
        mousemove: Ext.emptyFn,
        mouseenter: Ext.emptyFn,
        mouseleave: Ext.emptyFn,
        mousedown: Ext.emptyFn,
        mouseup: Ext.emptyFn
    }

});
```

This interaction leverages the existing itemhighlight interaction by extending the Ext.chart.interactions.ItemHighlight class. It uses the tap gesture, and hence sets the handlers for the other events to Ext.emptyFn so that those events will not have any effect if this custom ItemHighlight interaction is used.

Since the existing ItemHighlight interaction already watches for the tap event and fires the itemhighlight event when a series sprite is tapped, we did not have to do any more work in our class. However, in order to find out the series sprite that needs to be highlighted when the user taps on a chart, the itemhighlight interaction calls the getItemForPoint method on the series and passes the event position as its arguments. So, it is up to the series to return the sprite based on the passed event position.

Since our series—PeriodicTable—is a custom series that draws the sprites for elements; we need to implement the getItemForPoint method on this series so that it can return the matching sprite based on this custom logic. The next step shows the implementation of this method.

4. Edit the `app/series/PeriodicTable.js` file and add the following methods to it:

```
getItemForPoint: function (x, y) {
    if (this.getSprites()) {
        var me = this,
            sprite = me.getSprites()[0],
            store = me.getStore(),
            item, index;

        if (me.getHidden()) {
            return null;
        }
        if (sprite) {
            index = me.getIndexNearPoint(x, y);
            if (index !== -1) {
                item = {
                    series: me,
                    category: 'items',
                    index: index,
                    record: store.getData().items[index],
                    field: 'name',
                    sprite: sprite
                };
                return item;
            }
        }
    }
},

getIndexNearPoint: function(x, y) {
    var me = this;
    var tmp = null,
        items = me.sprites,
        i,
        l = items.length;

    for (i = 0; i < l; i++) {
        tmp = items[i];

        var attr = tmp.attr;

        if ((x >= attr.x && x <= (attr.x + attr.width)) &&
            (y >= attr.y && y <= (attr.y + attr.height))) {
```

```
            return i;
        }
    }
}
```

The `getItemForPoint` method must return an object with `series`, `category`, `index`, `record`, `field`, and `sprite` fields. This method identifies the matching sprite using the private method — `getIndexNearPoint`. If a valid index is returned, it forms the following object and returns it:

```
item = {
    series: me,
    category: 'items',
    index: index,
    record: store.getData().items[index],
    field: 'name',
    sprite: sprite
};
```

The returned object is passed as an argument to the `itemhighlight` event on the chart, which we will handle in the next step.

5. Edit the `app/view/Main.js` file and add the `sce-itemhighlight` interaction to the PeriodicTable chart, as highlighted here in bold:

```
items: [{
    xtype: 'periodictable',
    interactions: ['sce-itemhighlight'],
...

listeners: {
    itemhighlight: function(itemSelected) {
        if (itemSelected && itemSelected.record) {
            alert('Selected element is: ' + itemSelected.record.
get(itemSelected.field));
        }
    }
}
```

6. Run the application inside your browser and you will be able to see the element's name in an alert when you tap on a PeriodicTable element.

So, we saw how powerful interactions can be and how neatly they can be implemented to bring in the much needed analysis power to our charts. Like any other class in Sencha Ext JS or Touch frameworks, interaction-related classes can also be created from scratch; alternatively, classes can be created by extending an existing interaction or by overriding an existing interaction.

Summary

In this chapter, you learned how Sencha Charts offers interaction classes to build interactivity into the charts. We looked at the out-of-the-box interactions, their specific configurations, and how to use them on different types of charts. We also discussed how gestures are used in interactions and how to use this mechanism to develop custom interactions for cartesian, polar, and spacefilling charts.

This brings us to the end of our discussion on the Sencha Charts package. In the next chapter, we will look into some of the other popular JavaScript charting libraries and see how they fair with Sencha Charts.

Comparison with Other JavaScript Charting Libraries

9

Besides Sencha Charts, there are various other charting libraries that are popular and in use. Each library offers a charting capability in its own unique way. In this chapter, we will talk about the following charting libraries and see how we can create a chart similar to what we created in *Chapter 7*, *Theming*, using Sencha Charts:

- Google Charts
- FusionCharts
- amCharts
- HighCharts

This chapter will not recommend which charting library you should use, rather, it will only showcase how the respective charting APIs can be used to create a chart, which will give you an idea about the development approach that you will need when you intend to use a particular library. It will also give you an idea about how these approaches and APIs differ from those of Sencha Charts.

In *Chapter 7, Theming,* we produced the following chart using the Sencha Charts library:

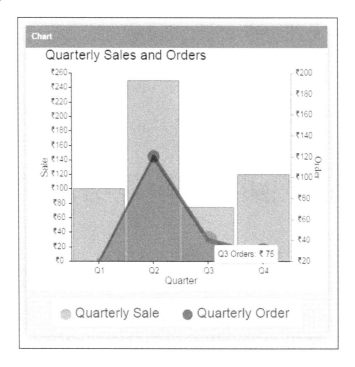

Looking at this chart, we can derive the following requirements for our chart, which we will try to achieve using the different charting libraries:

- A chart with a title
- Two series — bar and area
- Series having their own color pallet
- Two *y* axes with labels
- *y* axes labels with the rupee symbol
- The right-hand side *y* axis line in red color
- A tooltip showing sales/orders amount for a quarter
- Area series with circular markers of varying radius and color
- Emphasis on a certain part of an order area chart where the lines are drawn in bold with varying line width
- A legend with styled background

With these requirements in place, let's start with the libraries and create a similar looking chart. We will try to be as close as possible to the preceding chart using the out-of-the-box capabilities of the charting libraries.

 When you checkout the code from the GitHub repository, code related to this chapter is located under the ch09 folder.

Google Charts

Google Charts is a data visualization library from Google. It renders charts using SVG and VML (for older IE versions), and offers cross-platform portability to iPhones, iPads, and Android.

Let's follow these steps to create the desired chart using Google Charts:

1. Create the ch09/GoogleCharts folder.

2. Create the index.html file and save the following code in it:

```
<html>
  <head>
    <script type="text/javascript" src="https://www.google.com/jsapi"></script>

    <script type="text/javascript" src="app.js"></script>
  </head>

  <body>
    <div id="chartdiv" style="width:600; height:500"></div>
  </body>
</html>
```

3. Create the app.js file and save the following code in it:

```
google.load('visualization', '1.0', {'packages':['corechart']});

// Set a callback to run when the Google Visualization API is
loaded.
google.setOnLoadCallback(drawChart);

function drawChart() {

        var data = new google.visualization.arrayToDataTable([
```

```
            ['Month', 'Sales', {role: 'tooltip'}, 'Order', {role:
    'tooltip'}, {role: 'emphasis'}, {'type': 'string', 'role':
    'style'}],
            ['Q1', 100, 'Q1 Sales: \u20B9100', 20, 'Q1 Orders: \
    u20B920', false, 'point { size: 10; fill-color: red }'],
            ['Q2', 250, 'Q2 Sales: \u20B9250', 120, 'Q2 Orders: \
    u20B9120', false, 'point { size: 60; fill-color: black }'],
            ['Q3', 75, 'Q3 Sales: \u20B975', 40, 'Q3 Orders: \
    u20B940', true, 'point { size: 20; fill-color: red }'],
            ['Q4', 120, 'Q4 Sales: \u20B9120', 25, 'Q4 Orders: \
    u20B925', true, 'point { size: 15; fill-color: black }']
        ]);

    var options = {
      colors: ['#94AE0A', '#486989'],
      title: 'Quarterly Sales and Orders',
      titleTextStyle: {
        fontSize: 22
      },
      animation: {
        startup: true,
        easing: 'in',
        duration: 1000
      },
      legend: {
        alignment: 'center',
        position: 'bottom',
        textStyle: {
          fontSize: 22
        }
      },
      series: {
        0: { type: 'bars' , targetAxisIndex: 0 },
        1: { type: 'area', targetAxisIndex: 1}
      },
      hAxis: {
        title: 'Quarter',
        titleTextStyle: {
          color: 'red',
          italic: false,
          bold: true
        }
      },
```

```
        vAxes: {
          0: {
            title: 'Sales',
            titleTextStyle: {
              italic: false
            },
            format: "\u20B9 #,###"
          },
          1: {
            title: 'Order',
            titleTextStyle: {
              italic: false
            },
            format: "\u20B9 #,###"
          }
        },
        pointSize: 10,
        dataOpacity: 0.3,
        areaOpacity: 0.5,
        fontSize: 14
      };

    var chart = new google.visualization.ComboChart(document.
getElementById('chartdiv'));
      chart.draw(data, options);
}
```

The preceding code creates a chart using the Google Charts APIs. The
google.load asynchronously loads the Visualization library. As soon as
the loading is completed, it calls the drawChart method, which is registered
as the OnLoad callback using the setOnLoadCallback method. These are
standard lines of code that apply to creating any chart using Google Charts.

The drawChart method is where the all the action happens. Data defines a
DataTable with columns and rows, which is used to feed data to the two
series—bars and area. To show the tooltip for the sales and order series,
we have added two columns with role set as tooltip. Based on this role,
the Visualization library will pull out the column data to create the tooltip
content for the series points.

To emphasize a certain part of the order series, we added a column with
role set as emphasis and passed a true value to show the part of the order
series with a wider line.

The `options` object describes the chart configuration with which, the `ComboChart` is drawn and rendered as a child element of the `chartdiv div` element.

The last column in the `DataTable` is defined as a column with the `style` role. This allows us to control the point marker where we specified the radius of the circular marker using `size` and its color using `fill-color`.

A series is associated with one of the *y* axes using the `targetAxisIndex` property.

Deploy the code in web server and access `index.html` in your browser that supports SVG. You will see the following output:

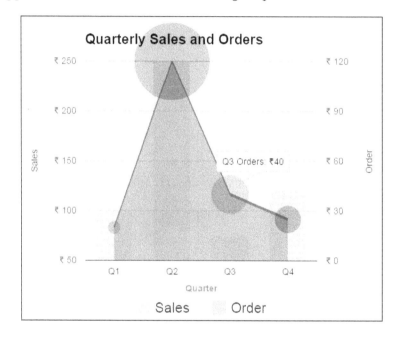

There is no direct way to draw the lines for *y* axes. However, with gridlines, we can make it easier for the user to identify the value for a point.

FusionCharts

This is one of the most comprehensive open charting libraries in terms of different types of charts supported by a JS charting library. Like Google Charts, FusionCharts also renders charts using SVG and VML.

We will create the chart based on the following steps:

1. Create the `ch09/FusionCharts` folder.

2. Create the `index.html` file and save the following code in it:

```
<!DOCTYPE html PUBLIC "-//W3C//DTD XHTML 1.0 Transitional//EN"
"http://www.w3.org/TR/xhtml1/DTD/xhtml1-transitional.dtd">
<html xmlns="http://www.w3.org/1999/xhtml">
<head>
  <title>FusionCharts</title>
  <meta http-equiv="Content-Type" content="text/html;
charset=UTF-8">

  <script src="sdk/js/fusioncharts.js"></script>
  <script type="text/javascript" src="sdk/js/themes/fusioncharts.
theme.fint.js"></script>

  <script type="text/javascript" src="themes/awesome.js"></script>
  <script type="text/javascript" src="app_themed.js"></script>

</head>

<body>
  <div id="chartdiv"></div>
</body>
</html>
```

The `fusioncharts.js` file contains the library and `fusioncharts.theme.fint.js` is one of the themes. The document body contains a `div` where the chart will be rendered.

Now, let's define the theme.

3. Create the `themes/awesome.js` file and save the following code in it:

```
FusionCharts.register("theme",{
  name: "awesome",
  theme: {
        base: {
          chart:{
                "captionPadding": "40",
                "numberPrefix": "₹",
                "sNumberPrefix": "₹",
                "showBorder": "0",
                "showValues": "0",
                "paletteColors": "#94AE0A,#486989",
```

```
                               "baseFontSize": "14",
                               "bgColor": "#ffffff",
                               "showCanvasBorder": "0",
                               "canvasBgAlpha": "0",
                               "captionAlignment": "left",
                               "captionFontSize": "22",
                               "showXAxisLine": "1",
                               "xAxisLineThickness": "1",
                               "xAxisLineColor": "#999999",
                               "showAlternateHGridColor": "0",
                               "usePlotGradientColor": "0",
                               "plotHoverEffect": "1",
                               "drawAnchors": "1",
                               "anchorRadius": 10,
                               "anchorBgColor": '#F78181',
                               "anchorBgAlpha": "30",
                               "anchorAlpha": "100",
                               "legendBgColor": "#FBEFF2",
                               "legendBorderColor": '#CCCCCC',
                               "legendItemFontSize": '22'
                        }
                  }
            }
});
```

In the preceding code, we defined a theme for our chart and registered it with FusionCharts with the name `awesome`. We defined the colors for the two series using `paletteColors`. The marker's look and feel is controlled using the various **Anchor** properties. The chart title is styled using **Caption** properties.

The `numberPrefix` value is used to prefix the number value with the rupee symbol on the primary *y* axis — **Sales**, which is rendered on the left-hand side, whereas `sNumberPrefix` is used to format the number on the secondary *y* axis — **Orders**, which is rendered on the right-hand side.

There is no direct property available to style the primary and secondary *y* axes lines.

With the theme in place, we will now create the chart using it.

4. Create the `app_themed.js` file and save the following code in it:

```
FusionCharts.ready(function () {
    var salesAnlysisChart = new FusionCharts({
        type: 'mscombidy2d',
        renderAt: 'chartdiv',
```

```
width: '600',
height: '500',
dataFormat: 'json',
dataSource: {
    "chart": {
        "theme": "awesome",
        "caption": "Quarterly Sales and Orders",
        "xAxisname": "Quarter",
        "pYAxisName": "Sales",
        "sYAxisName": "Order"
    },
    "categories": [
        {
            "category": [
                {
                    "label": "Q1"
                },
                {
                    "label": "Q2"
                },
                {
                    "label": "Q3"
                },
                {
                    "label": "Q4"
                }
            ]
        }
    ],
    "dataset": [
        {
            "seriesName": "Sales",
            "data": [
                {
                    "value": 100
                },
                {
                    "value": 250
                },
                {
                    "value": 75
                },
```

```
                        {
                            "value": 120
                        }
                    ]
                },
                {
                    "seriesName": "Order",
                    "parentYAxis": "S",
                    "renderAs": "area",
                    "data": [
                        {
                            "value": 20,
                            "anchorRadius": "10",
                            "anchorBgColor": "#FF0000"
                        },
                        {
                            "value": 120,
                            "anchorRadius": "60",
                            "anchorBgColor": "#000000"
                        },
                        {
                            "value": 40,
                            "anchorRadius": "20",
                            "anchorBgColor": "#FF0000"
                        },
                        {
                            "value": 25,
                            "anchorRadius": "15",
                            "anchorBgColor": "#000000"
                        }
                    ]
                }
            ]
        }
    }).render();
});
```

In the preceding code, we instantiated the FusionCharts class with the mscombidy2d type chart as it supports column charts, line charts, area charts, and dual *y* axis, which is close to what we need for our chart where we have a column chart, an area chart, and two *y* axes. The renderAt method tells the FusionCharts class where to render the chart.

FusionCharts supports XML as well as JSON to describe a chart. In this case, we used JSON by setting `dataFormat` to `json`. The `dataSource` contains the JSON description of our chart. The description starts with the `chart` config where the chart title, theme, *x* axis, primary *y* axis, and secondary *y* axis are described.

The `categories` defines the category data that will be used to create values for *x* axis.

The `dataset` contains two series—`column` and `area`. Since `column` is the default series type, we did not have to set `renderAs` on the first series object. Each series has its `data` that it uses to create the respective axis labels, point values, and tooltips. For `Order` series, the data contains `anchorRadius` and `anchorBgColor` to draw a marker/anchor with different dimensions and colors. Unlike Sencha Charts, there is no way to derive this information at runtime, unless the data is created at runtime.

> The properties that we have used in defining the theme are the properties that can be passed to the `chart` config while instantiating a `FusionCharts` object. You can refer to the `ch09/FusionCharts/app.js` file to see this in action.

Running the application in the browser will produce the following output:

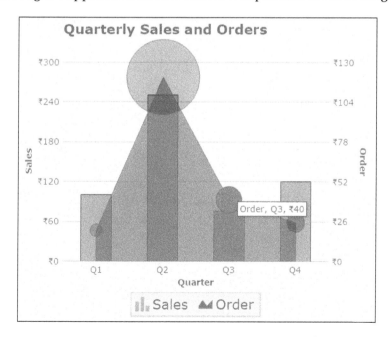

amCharts

amCharts is a responsive modern charting library that renders charts using SVG and is supported by touch or mobile devices.

Let's create the chart by performing the following steps:

1. Create the `ch09/amCharts` folder.

2. Create the `index.html` file and save the following code inside it:

```
<!DOCTYPE html PUBLIC "-//W3C//DTD XHTML 1.0 Transitional//EN"
"http://www.w3.org/TR/xhtml1/DTD/xhtml1-transitional.dtd">
<html xmlns="http://www.w3.org/1999/xhtml">
<head>
  <title>amCharts</title>
  <meta http-equiv="Content-Type" content="text/html;
charset=UTF-8">
  <script type="text/javascript" src="http://www.amcharts.com/
lib/3/amcharts.js"></script>
  <script type="text/javascript" src="http://www.amcharts.com/
lib/3/serial.js"></script>
  <script type="text/javascript" src="http://www.amcharts.com/
lib/3/themes/none.js"></script>

  <script type="text/javascript" src="themes/awesome.js"></script>

  <script type="text/javascript" src="app_themed.js"></script>

  <style>
    #chartdiv{
      width: 600px;
      height: 500px;
    }

    #chartdiv .amcharts-legend-div {
      background-color: #DCDCDC;
    }
  </style>
</head>

<body>
  <div id="chartdiv"></div>
</body>

</html>
```

3. Create the `themes/awesome.js` file and save the following code inside it:

```
AmCharts.themes.awesome = {

  themeName: "awesome",

  AmChart: {
    fontSize: 14
  },

  Title: {
    size: 22
  },

  AmGraph: {
    fillAlphas: 0.7,
    fillColors: "#94AE0A",
    lineColor: "#566606"
  },

  AxisBase: {
    gridAlpha: 0
  },

  ValueAxis: {
    axisColor: 'red'
  },

  ChartCursor: {
    cursorColor: "#000000",
    color: "#FFFFFF",
    cursorAlpha: 0.1
  },

  AmLegend: {
    backgroundColor: "#FBEFF2",
    backgroundAlpha: 0.7,
    fontSize: 11
  }
};
```

The preceding code defines the awesome theme for our chart that we will be creating in the next step. The AmChart contains the chart-level configuration. The Title contains the configuration related to the chart title. The AmGraph configuration applies to all the series in the chart. The AxisBase configuration applies to **Category** as well as **Value** axes, whereas the ValueAxis configuration applies to just the value axis where we show the numbers or facts—**Sales** and **Orders**.

The configs—AxisBase, ValueAxis, AmLegend, and so on, are the class names in the amCharts library and their properties are those class attributes.

4. Create the app_themed.js file and save the following code in it:

```
var chart = AmCharts.makeChart("chartdiv", {
    "type": "serial",
    "theme": "awesome",
    "creditsPosition": "bottom-right",
    "titles": [
        {
            "size": 22,
            "text": "Quarterly Sales and Orders"
        }
    ],
    "legend": {
        "equalWidths": false,
        "useGraphSettings": true,
        "valueAlign": "left",
        "valueWidth": 80,
        "periodValueText": "Total: ₹ [[value.sum]]"
    },
    "dataProvider": [
        { month: 'Q1', sales: 100, order: 20 },
        { month: 'Q2', sales: 250, order: 120 },
        { month: 'Q3', sales: 75, order: 40},
        { month: 'Q4', sales: 120, order: 25}
    ],
    "valueAxes": [{
        "id": "salesAxis",
        "position": "left",
        "title": "Sales",
        "labelFunction": function(value, valueText, valueAxis) {
            return "₹ " + value;
        }
```

```
}, {
    "id": "orderAxis",
    "position": "right",
    "title": "Order",
    "labelFunction": function(value, valueText, valueAxis) {
        return "₹ " + value;
    }
}],
"graphs": [{
    "balloonText": "[[month]] Sales: ₹ [[value]]",
    "dashLengthField": "dashLength",
    "legendValueText": "[[month]]: ₹ [[value]]",
    "title": "Sales",
    "type": "column",
    "valueField": "sales",
    "valueAxis": "salesAxis"
}, {
    "balloonText": "[[month]] Orders: ₹ [[value]]",
    "bullet": "round",
    "bulletAlpha": 0.4,
    "bulletBorderAlpha": 1,
    "useLineColorForBulletBorder": true,
    "bulletSizeField": "order",
    "dashLengthField": "dashLength",
    "legendValueText": "[[month]]: ₹ [[value]]",
    "title": "Order",
    "fillAlphas": 0.4,
    "valueField": "order",
    "valueAxis": "orderAxis",
    "fillColors": "red",
    "lineColor": "#486989"
}],
"chartCursor": {
    "fullWidth":true,
    "valueBalloonsEnabled": false,
    "zoomable": false
},
"dataDateFormat": "YYYY-MM-DD",
"categoryField": "month"
});
```

The preceding code creates an instance of `AmChart` with two *y* axes using the `valueAxes` configuration. Two series are added to the `graphs` configuration. A series is linked to an axis using the `valueAxis` property. The tooltip text is controlled using `balloonText`. Markers are controlled using various Bullet-related properties.

The properties used in the theme definition can, as well, be passed to their respective configuration objects. For example, `fontSize: 11` can be passed to the `"legend"` configuration object. You can refer to the `ch09/amCharts/app.js` file to see how this is done.

The following shows the output produced by the preceding code:

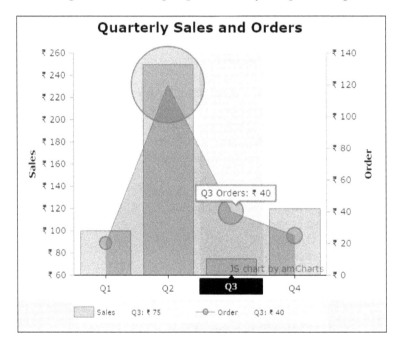

HighCharts

Like other JS charting libraries that we talked about, HighCharts also renders charts using SVG. We will create the desired chart using this library using the following steps:

1. Create the `ch09/HighCharts` folder.

2. Create the `index.html` file and save the following code in it:

```html
<!DOCTYPE html PUBLIC "-//W3C//DTD XHTML 1.0 Transitional//EN"
"http://www.w3.org/TR/xhtml1/DTD/xhtml1-transitional.dtd">
<html xmlns="http://www.w3.org/1999/xhtml">
<head>
  <title>HighCharts</title>
  <meta http-equiv="Content-Type" content="text/html;
charset=UTF-8">

  <script src="//code.jquery.com/jquery-1.11.2.min.js"></script>
  <script src="//code.jquery.com/jquery-migrate-1.2.1.min.js"></
script>

  <script src="http://code.highcharts.com/highcharts.js"></script>

  <script type="text/javascript" src="themes/awesome.js"></script>
  <script type="text/javascript" src="app_themed.js"></script>

  <style>
    #chartdiv{
      width: 600px;
      height: 500px;
    }
  </style>
</head>

<body>
  <div id="chartdiv"></div>
</body>
</html>
```

We included jQuery files as HighCharts uses it for DOM manipulation. In the next step, we will define the `awesome` theme for our HighCharts instance.

3. To define the theme, create the `themes/awesome.js` file and save the following code in it:

```javascript
Highcharts.theme = {
  colors: ['#94AE0A', '#486989'],
  chart: {
    backgroundColor: null
  },
    credits: {
      enabled: false
    },
```

```
title: {
  style: {
    color: 'black',
    fontSize: '22px',
    fontWeight: 'bold'
  }
},
tooltip: {
  borderWidth: 0
},
legend: {
  backgroundColor: '#F2EAEC',
  itemStyle: {
    fontWeight: 'bold',
    fontSize: '13px'
  }
},
xAxis: {
  lineColor: '#333'
},
yAxis: {
  lineColor: '#333',
  tickColor: '#333',
  labels: {
    style: {
      color: '#333'
    }
  }
},
plotOptions: {
  series: {
    shadow: true
  }
}
};

// Apply the theme
Highcharts.setOptions(Highcharts.theme);
```

The configs that we have specified above are applied to the chart, directly, using the setOptions API.

4. Create the `app_themed.js` file and save the following code inside it:

```
$(function () {
    new Highcharts.Chart({

        chart: {
            renderTo: 'chartdiv'
        },

        title: {
            text: 'Quarterly Sales and Orders'
        },

        xAxis: {
            categories: ['Q1', 'Q2', 'Q3', 'Q4'],
            title: 'Quarters',
            labels: {
                format: '{value}'
            }
        },

        yAxis: [{
            tickWidth: 1,
            gridLineWidth: 0,
            allowDecimals: false,
            min: 0,
            lineWidth: 1,
            title: {
                text: 'Sales'
            },
            labels: {
                format: '₹ {value}'
            }
        }, {
            tickWidth: 1,
            gridLineWidth: 0,
            lineColor: 'red',
            tickColor: 'red',
            allowDecimals: false,
            min: 0,
            lineWidth: 1,
            title: {
                text: 'Orders'
            },
```

```
            opposite: true,
            labels: {
                format: '₹ {value}'
            }
        }],

        tooltip: {
            formatter: function () {
                return this.point.name + ' ' + this.series.name +
': ₹' + this.y;
            }
        },

        plotOptions: {
            area: {
                fillOpacity: 0.3
            }
        },

        series: [{
            type: 'column',
            name: 'Sales',
            yAxis: 0,
            data: [{
                name: 'Q1',
                type: 'category',
                y: 100
            }, {
                name: 'Q2',
                type: 'category',
                y: 250
            }, {
                name: 'Q3',
                type: 'category',
                y: 75
            }, {
                name: 'Q4',
                type: 'category',
                y: 120
            }],
            style: {
                color: 'red'
            }
```

```
        }, {
            type: 'area',
            name: 'Orders',
            yAxis: 1,
            data: [{
                name: 'Q1',
                type: 'category',
                y: 20,
                marker: {
                    radius: 8
                }
            }, {
                name: 'Q2',
                type: 'category',
                y: 120,
                marker: {
                    radius: 24,
                    states: {
                        hover: {
                            radius: 28
                        }
                    }
                }
            }, {
                name: 'Q3',
                type: 'category',
                y: 40,
                marker: {
                    radius: 16
                }
            }, {
                name: 'Q4',
                type: 'category',
                y: 25,
                marker: {
                    radius: 10
                }
            }]
        }]
    });
});
```

The preceding code creates a `HighCharts` instance, as shown here. The *x* axis data — **Quarters** — is added to the `xAxis` config using the `categories` property whereas **Sales** and **Order** data is mentioned as `y` property on each *y* axis' `data` object.

The marker's radius is controlled using the `marker` configuration on the `data` object for each point.

Refer to the `ch09/HighCharts/app.js` file to see how the properties used in defining the theme can be set directly on the `HighCharts` instance, as well.

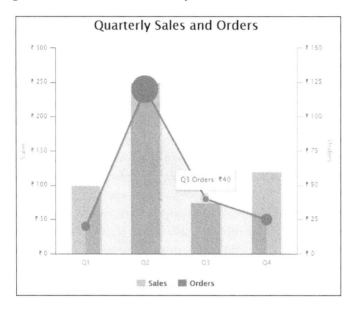

Summary

We started this book with a discussion on the SVG and Canvas APIs and you learned about the fundamentals of charting. After that, you learned about the Sencha Charts package and created different types of interactive charts using its out-of-the-box capabilities. Next, you learned about creating custom cartesian, polar, and spacefilling charts and also created gestures-based custom interactions. Finally, we saw how to style and theme a Sencha Charts-based chart.

In this chapter, we took a Sencha Charts-based chart, which we had created earlier, as a case study and tried to create a similar chart using various, popularly used JavaScript charting libraries — Google Charts, FusionCharts, amCharts, and HighCharts. It showed how the libraries differ in terminologies, APIs, properties, theming mechanism, and customization possibilities. This will help us to compare different charting libraries and see how they fair with Sencha Charts.

Index

A

B

C

Thank you for buying
Sencha Charts Essentials

About Packt Publishing

Packt, pronounced 'packed', published its first book, *Mastering phpMyAdmin for Effective MySQL Management*, in April 2004, and subsequently continued to specialize in publishing highly focused books on specific technologies and solutions.

Our books and publications share the experiences of your fellow IT professionals in adapting and customizing today's systems, applications, and frameworks. Our solution-based books give you the knowledge and power to customize the software and technologies you're using to get the job done. Packt books are more specific and less general than the IT books you have seen in the past. Our unique business model allows us to bring you more focused information, giving you more of what you need to know, and less of what you don't.

Packt is a modern yet unique publishing company that focuses on producing quality, cutting-edge books for communities of developers, administrators, and newbies alike. For more information, please visit our website at www.packtpub.com.

About Packt Open Source

In 2010, Packt launched two new brands, Packt Open Source and Packt Enterprise, in order to continue its focus on specialization. This book is part of the Packt Open Source brand, home to books published on software built around open source licenses, and offering information to anybody from advanced developers to budding web designers. The Open Source brand also runs Packt's Open Source Royalty Scheme, by which Packt gives a royalty to each open source project about whose software a book is sold.

Writing for Packt

We welcome all inquiries from people who are interested in authoring. Book proposals should be sent to author@packtpub.com. If your book idea is still at an early stage and you would like to discuss it first before writing a formal book proposal, then please contact us; one of our commissioning editors will get in touch with you.

We're not just looking for published authors; if you have strong technical skills but no writing experience, our experienced editors can help you develop a writing career, or simply get some additional reward for your expertise.

Creating Mobile Apps with Sencha Touch 2

ISBN: 978-1-84951-890-1   Paperback: 348 pages

Learn to use the Sencha Touch programming language and expand your skills by building 10 unique applications

1. Learn the Sencha Touch programming language by building real, working applications.

2. Each chapter focuses on different features and programming approaches; you can decide which is right for you.

3. Full of well-explained example code and rich with screenshots.

Sencha MVC Architecture

ISBN: 978-1-84951-888-8   Paperback: 126 pages

A practical guide for designers and developers to create scalable enterprise-class web applications in ExtJS and Sencha Touch using the Sencha MVC architecture

1. Map general MVC architecture concept to the classes in ExtJS 4.x and Sencha Touch.

2. Create a practical application in ExtJS as well as Sencha Touch using various Sencha MVC architecture concepts and classes.

3. Dive deep into the building blocks of the Sencha MVC architecture including the class system, loader, controller, and application.

Please check **www.PacktPub.com** for information on our titles

Learning Ext JS 4

ISBN: 978-1-84951-684-6   Paperback: 434 pages

Sencha Ext JS for a beginner

1. Learn the basics and create your first classes.

2. Handle data and understand the way it works, create powerful widgets and new components.

3. Dig into the new architecture defined by Sencha and work on real-world projects.

Ext JS 4 Web Application Development Cookbook

ISBN: 978-1-84951-686-0   Paperback: 488 pages

Over 110 easy-to-follow recipes backed up with real-life examples, walking you through basic Ext JS features to advanced application design using Sencha's Ext JS

1. Learn how to build Rich Internet applications with the latest version of the Ext JS framework in a cookbook style.

2. From creating forms to theming your interface, you will learn the building blocks for developing the perfect web application.

3. Easy to follow recipes step through practical and detailed examples which are all fully backed up with code, illustrations, and tips.

Please check **www.PacktPub.com** for information on our titles

www.ingramcontent.com/pod-product-compliance
Lightning Source LLC
Chambersburg PA
CBHW060557060326
40690CB00017B/3738